COSTUME JEWELRY IN VOGUE

JANE MULVAGH

COSTUME JEWELRY IN VOGUE

PREFACE BY

PALOMA PICASSO

With 345 illustrations, 64 in color

THAMES AND HUDSON

For Christine Blackwell

Acknowledgments

In starting to research this book I was immensely grateful to those who shared their knowledge and opened their address books, including Valerie Mendes of the Victoria and Albert Museum, Akoushla Hicks of Grays, Veronica Manussis of Cobra & Bellamy and Simon Wilson of Butler & Wilson.

Kenneth Snowman and Geoffrey Munn of Wartski, Mark Evans of Bentleys and Gordon Watson of Lewis Kaplan all provided me with specialist information, while the technical information about the industry was gleaned from Francis and Marcel Mann, of Adrian Mann Ltd, Hugh Allen of Trifari, Don McDonald of Walter Scaife, Otto Koeppen of Grossé/Dior and Mr Benson of Napier Inc.

The varied uses of costume jewelry in a fashion collection were learnt from Louise de la Falaise at Yves Saint Laurent, Dominique Sirop at Givenchy, and Geoffrey Beene and Ken Lane, whose opinions and memories I valued.

Stefan Wagstyl at the *Financial Times* provided me with impeccable information about the precious metal markets. I thank him.

Robert Lee Morris of Artwear gave me a fascinating insight into both the art and industry of costume jewelry, while M. Goossens of Goossens in Paris shared his knowledge about the craftsmanship of the business and his remembrances of Chanel, Balenciaga and Dior. I thoroughly enjoyed learning from them both.

Billyboy! Together we chuckled and gasped our way through his outstanding collection of period costume jewelry. And the stories he had to tell!... Thank you. He also provided the pictures of Surrealist jewelry from his own collection, for which we are very grateful.

The Book Department at Condé Nast have been tremendously helpful and fun to work with: Robin Muir for his copy editing; Jane Ross for her picture research and captioning; Jane Meakin, the librarian; and Sara Longworth for her tireless help and gracious smiles, no matter what scowls she was presented with. I thank also Alex Kroll for his tolerant and friendly advice as Editor, Condé Nast Books, and Elizabeth Wickham for her witty designing, patience and friendship. Madeleine Parrish of American *Vogue* was a welcoming and informative colleague in New York.

Finally, I would like to thank all those at Thames and Hudson with whom I had the pleasure of working.

Designed by Elizabeth Wickham

First published in the United States in 1988 by
Thames and Hudson Inc., 500 Fifth Avenue,
New York, New York 10110

Library of Congress Catalog Card Number 88-50192

Printed and bound in Japan by Dai Nippon

Title page Ken Lane's twisted strands of coloured beads forming bracelets fastened with enamel clasps; Hattie Carnegie's rhinestone bangle and Ben-King's black satin belt studded with rhinestones slung over a black wool dress, 1965. Irving Penn

CONTENTS

Preface

PALOMA PICASSO

Real or fake, does it really matter? It is the beauty that counts: the boldness, the colours, the effect. In fact, the fear of using expensive materials can be very limiting, especially on size. And I love size. Big, bold, smooth shapes.

I'm a great believer in accessories, and costume jewelry is the most versatile one. Simple fashion demands important jewelry, but during periods when clothes become more ornate, it tends to be ousted by the decorative details of the clothing. But it *always* comes back and is always worth keeping. Clothes date much faster than *bijoux fantasie*. Costume jewelry is timeless, fun, expressive. That attracts me.

When you wear black, you can use lots of accessories. If you wear prints, it's harder to mix accessories. And I think accessories make dressing amusing. I've always loved jewelry, which is why I've ended up designing it.

Like any child, baubles had attracted me from an early age. I remember imploring my mother to give me this or that piece when she tired of it. I recall the thrill of arriving in Venice and searching out the most colourful Murano glass beads. How I loved those sparkling colours round my neck as a child – and I still do.

As an assistant to a stage designer working on the play *Madame* in Paris I was asked to find some eye-catching jewelry for the heroine to wear. Having searched the city's junk shops high and low, it seemed that the only answer was to make it myself. Delving into the costume trunks, scrabbling around on the theatre floor, I found some beads and mischievously picked out diamanté and coloured glass stones from the corsets of the *Folies Bergère* outfits. I made an enormous choker on a black velvet ribbon. And Oh, the thrill of having my jewelry mentioned in a critic's review. It was only later that I realized it was because of my name. Have you ever heard of the jewelry designer getting a mention in a review?

I decided to go to jewelry design school and make some costume jewelry since I already had the publicity. But how was I to price my collection of trinkets? The components were valueless and would anyone buy them? Again, chance provided an answer. While dining in a restaurant with my box of junk beside me I spotted Yves Saint Laurent. So I rushed over to show him my jewels. I thought, he'll know what it's worth. How naive I was – he hadn't a clue. You see Yves understands beauty, not pricing strategies! But on the strength of our rendezvous he invited me to design jewels for his fashion collection.

I collect accessories – lots of jewelry – real or fake, because I like big jewelry, even though I am small. Little jewelry does not work for me. It's a question of bones and proportion rather than of being small or tall. I've always been rather surprised that when I put a hat or jewel on, it's the bigger the better. I can't go half way. It has to be all or nothing.

Above Paloma Picasso's pink plastic rose is teamed with Ugo Correani's pink plastic rose hairpiece to accessorize Lancetti's maribou feather bolero, 1972. *Chris von Wangenheim*

Opposite Paloma Picasso, wearing her own jewelry for Tiffany's, 1984. *Tony Viramontes*

Introduction

The Origins of the Craft

'Vulgarity is a very important ingredient in life. I'm a great believer in vulgarity – if it's got vitality. A little bad taste is like a nice splash of paprika. We all need a splash of bad taste – it's hearty, it's physical. I think we could use more of it. No taste is what I'm against.'

Diana Vreeland

Costume jewelry has to be vital, fantastic, bold, for restraint has nothing to do with either the making or the wearing of it. Whereas imitation jewelry is applauded for its deceptive ingenuity rather than its artistry, costume jewelry is valued for its creative vigour and largesse. The most effective costume jewelry resists the temptation to look real; its frank fakery allows for a boldness of imagery that can even overshadow the clothes themselves.

The rôle of costume jewelry in fashion can be likened to that of the courtesan in society; she, as an outsider, unleashed from a strict social code, can afford to be – is expected to be – striking, risqué and exciting, whereas her social climbing sister, imitation jewelry, must be ever mindful of propriety and cautious not to offend.

The development of costume jewelry is inextricably linked with the history of dress, for its very purpose is to enhance the clothes that it accompanies, rather than to proclaim the wearer's wealth or status. The transitory nature of costume jewelry distinguishes it further; its effectiveness endures only as long as the fashion it complements.

There are many who produce costume jewelry but few who create it, and a clear distinction must be made between the two. Although designers in couture houses, or craftsmen employed by them, may introduce a style, it is the factories that mass-produce and popularize a look. This partnership – often a silent one – between couturier and artisan is mutually beneficial; the former benefits from good and novel design, which enhances a collection, while the latter is assured of a market and even of assistance in paying for the surprisingly expensive raw materials and processes. However, confusion

Opposite 'Black' painted woman wearing a Zulu necklace, 1967. *Serge Lutens*

has frequently arisen because couturiers suppress the designer's name, passing designs off as their own.

There is also, inevitably, an interplay between the 'créateur' and the 'façonnier'. In addition, the major fashion houses liaise with licensed manufacturers, who mass-produce and market a look across the world under a designer's label. Grossé's work for Dior and Monet's arrangement with Yves Saint Laurent are classic examples today.

Parure of paste and jargoons in closed silver settings; strass necklace, pendant earrings, aigrette and brooch, c 1770. *Courtesy of Christie's, London*

The craft of costume jewelry originated not in the fine jewelry houses but in the fashion ateliers, where craftsmen used strass, paste, semi-precious stones and bugle beads to ornament bodices, berthas, shoe buckles, haircombs and handbag clasps for the couture. Glass was an important constituent of many of these decorative pieces and consequently the development of glass production was essential to the founding of the craft of bead and jewelry-making.

The ancient Egyptians were the first to produce glass; according to the Egyptologist Sir W. M. Flinders Petrie, they started to glaze stone beads in around 12,000 BC, and were producing glass objects from 7000 BC onward. Since glass was expensive and difficult to manufacture, the Egyptians considered it to be as valuable as rare, natural gems and, as a result, used it almost exclusively for personal adornment.

The Romans acquired many of the Egyptian glass-making techniques which were, in turn, passed on to the Venetians. From the eleventh century the Venetian doges guarded these skills, passing draconian laws to prevent glass-making secrets from leaving the country. In 1291 the glass ovens were moved from Venice to the neighbouring island of Murano and by the fifteenth century the Italians had invented 'cristallo', a clear glass.

The Venetian monopoly was broken by the Englishman George Ravenscroft. With the help of an itinerant Italian glass-maker, Ravenscroft produced flint glass in 1675 and lead crystal in 1681. The lead crystal had a diamond-like sparkle which made it a suitable substitute for natural crystal. A little earlier, around 1600, the processes of cutting jewels and crystals had been applied to glass by Caspar Lehmann, the court jeweler to Emperor Rudolf II at Prague. By the 1780s Georges-Frédéric Strass had introduced glass paste jewelry (strass) to the novelty-hungry French court.

By the eighteenth century the Venetians' position as premier fine glass producer had been usurped by the Bohemians. Czechoslovakia has the longest tradition of glass bead production in the world: the first glass furnace was ignited in 1376 at Sklenarice, near Jablonec in north Bohemia, where the mountain water, sand and silicon deposits provided essential raw materials, and by the mid-sixteenth century a glassworks had been established at Mseno nad Nisou.

Opposite Portrait of Queen Elizabeth I, attributed to Nicholas Hilliard, c 1575, illustrating the Queen's use of gems – precious or cut glass – to ornament her clothing. *Courtesy of the National Portrait Gallery, London*

Originally the skills of stone-cutting were applied to the indigenous semi-precious stone deposits, such as agate. However, as stocks of these stones declined, alternatives were sought and in the eighteenth century a glass-stone-making industry developed.

At the beginning of the eighteenth century, the Germans, with their long history of metal-working skills, settled in Bohemia. The area could now produce not only cut-glass stones, but settings, claws, pins and chains as well. By the nineteenth century the Czechs virtually monopolized the production of cheap, cut-glass stones. They were hand-made by farmers who turned to this craft during the winter months – each farmhouse specializing in a particular type of stone. Middlemen travelled round the settlements collecting the wares and distributing them to a handful of exporters. The area became the main supplier of components, such as cut-stones, metal settings and imitation pearls, for the imitation jewelry and dress garniture workshops in Paris, Budapest and London.

The Czech and German inhabitants thrived side by side, supplying the world with glass beads. From the late nineteenth century craftsmen began to move out of the area. Daniel Swarovski, who was the first to produce jewelry stones by machine rather than by hand and who wanted to protect his secret, emigrated in 1895 to Wattens in the Austrian Tyrol, where 'white coal' (water power) and a huge labour force were available. His company developed a virtual monopoly of fine glass stone production and in the late 1890s started to produce jewelry.

It was the expansionist activities of Adolf Hitler in Sudetenland, northern Czechoslovakia, that finally dispersed the industry. The Jewish Germans and Czechs fled to Paris, London and New York, taking their skills, tool-making and stamping equipment with them. Other 'German' Czechs settled in Germany, many in Neugablonz. So one result of this diaspora was that there is invariably a Czechoslovakian immigrant behind every major costume jewelry or component firm in Europe or North America. Postwar Marshall Aid financed the establishment of many small glass-bead making factories throughout Europe. It also reconsolidated the industry in Czechoslovakia. The Czech industry was nationalized in 1948 and the export of all goods was united under one company, Jablonex. Today this firm employs more than 20,000 workers and is the biggest producer in the world. A *de facto* oligopoly of glass stone suppliers has consequently been established between Swarovski in Austria and Jablonex in Czechoslovakia.

Woman wiring up, prior to electro-plating, at the Trifari factory, c 1950. *Courtesy of Walter Scaife Ltd*

Within a hundred years the glass cutters of Bohemia and Silesia had achieved world prominence. An indication of the supremacy of Jablonex and Swarovski lies in a rumour that Japan had attempted to copy the glass-stone-cutting techniques of the Czechs. They failed, however, hampered not only by expense and production complications, but by the total market dominance of these two companies.

In order to create a glass bead, the glass is fashioned over fire-lamps on glass rods; the turning of the rod over the flame forms the bead. The bead can then be cut in one of three ways: with a diamond, with an amaril wheel (a hard, grinding wheel) or by machine. The latter method has gradually replaced the earlier hand methods, and the machine-cut stones that it produces are known as 'chatons'.

19th-century Berlin iron bracelet with fleur-de-lys links. *Courtesy of Christie's, London*

Imitation pearls, an important Czechoslovakian export, were first made in the fifteenth century and were used to embellish dresses and hats. They consisted of hollow glass beads filled with wax for weight. By the seventeenth century this type of pearl, the Roman pearl, was improved by adding a coating, known as *essence d'Orient*, to the inside of the glass bead, creating a nacreous effect. In Venetian pearls, introduced in the nineteenth century, this method was perfected by the application of *essence d'Orient* to the exterior of a solid glass bead.

Gradually craftsmen evolved their trade to suit a new demand – costume jewelry. The growth of this market was facilitated by three factors: first, the sartorial lead given by couturiers who sanctioned the use of trinket jewelry for fashionable effect; second, the acceptance of costume jewelry by leaders of society; and third, mechanization, which introduced ways of replacing the craftsman by the machine.

The use of 'valueless' materials for decorative and novel effect had been considered appropriate at various times throughout history but at no point was it related to seasonal fashion change. Elizabeth I, for instance, was occasionally known to adorn her dresses with stones – usually fine, and sometimes crude paste – while French court ladies were amused by the novelty of strass. Similarly, during the Napoleonic wars the patriotic bosoms of German ladies were hung with Berlin iron jewelry – intricate, filigree iron chains, crosses and medallions – proclaiming that they had surrendered their gems to raise money for the war effort. However, these items did not relate to fashionable dress.

Costume jewelry is in fact an entirely twentieth-century phenomenon; the term was first used in 1933 in the *New Yorker* magazine. Prior to that it had been referred to in *Vogue* as 'dress ornaments' or 'craftsmen's jewelry'. Various women's magazines were unequivocal about the wearing of sham jewelry; for example, *The Lady's Realm* of 1898 complained, '. . .the craze for imitation jewelry of a cheap kind is much to be deplored, for one reason – that it is so overdone. Little lace brooches, pins, etc., are charming, but we have often sighed to see otherwise well-dressed women spoilt by the donning of gim-crack chains, bracelets, etc.' Only when the leading couturiers

ordained that jewelry should become an intrinsic part of their collections, teaming an ensemble with a specific piece of costume jewelry, did a tradition grow, initially stunted by consumer conservatism.

Original, avant-garde costume jewelry is invariably created only because a single-minded fashion designer has accorded tremendous importance to it, not only as an accessory but as the very focal point of an ensemble, to which the clothes act merely as a backdrop.

Distinction must be made between recycled ideas and images and the truly original new shapes presented in novel materials and textures that so rarely emerge. Poiret's work with René Boivin; Chanel's with Gripoix and Count Etienne de Beaumont; Schiaparelli's with various Surrealist artists and jewelers such as Jean Schlumberger and Jean Clément; Giorgio di Sant' Angelo's work inspired by *Vogue*'s Diana Vreeland; Wendy Ramshaw's, Mick Milligan's and Andrew Logan's work in the late sixties and early seventies; the varied 'creative salvage' expressions of Judy Blame and other notable young Londoners in the eighties and Billyboy's witty interpretations of the spirit of Schiaparelli in modern resins; these are the true originals.

Most costume jewelry is simply a revamp of the old or a reinterpretation of 'fine' jewelry. The same ideas can be traced again and again throughout the decades; the gilt and *pâte de verre* style of Chanel and her associates in the late twenties and the thirties, for example, was revived following her comeback in the fifties and then parodied by Karl Lagerfeld in the eighties. Similarly, Schiaparelli's bizarre wit and Surrealism (considered very ugly, of '*mauvais caractère*', during the war and the postwar years when correct form and obvious feminine prettiness prevailed) enjoyed a renaissance in the

Above left Gabrielle Chanel with Salvador Dali, 1939

Centre Chanel's white jersey suit banded in navy-blue and worn with her gilt chain and medallion jewelry, 1958. *Henry Clarke*

Above Billyboy, hung with some of his Chanel-inspired costume jewelry collection, 1985. *Guy Aelbrecht for Regard's*

Opposite Chanel's timeless style: navy-blue and white striped cotton jersey tunic dress over a white pleated skirt, worn with a selection of gilt, medallion and pearl jewelry and matching belt, 1984. *Daniel Jouanneau*

Above Schiaparelli's porcelain vegetable bracelet, 1938

Below 1980s surrealism: Paul Monroe's rococo mirror with a tourist snap-shot of the Empire State Building, to be pinned to a lapel, 1985. *Andy Warhol, Randolph Grafe*

eighties, by which time a youthful and visually sophisticated generation was ready to enjoy her sartorial puns, shocking imagery and humorous artistry. In the same way, a link can be traced from Georg Jensen's futuristic jewelry of the first two decades of the century (when it was an expression of the Arts and Crafts movement, not a fashion accessory) and Modernist pieces which became fashionable in the thirties. This mood was reiterated in the seventies by Elsa Peretti and Paloma Picasso of Tiffany's, New York, and Robert Lee Morris for Artwear.

There are two methods by which metal components of costume jewelry are made – stamping and casting. Stamping is the older method. It is more precise than casting. Casting is a process by which metal shapes are formed by pouring molten metal into a mould. Originally, hand-carved, stone moulds were used, but these were superseded by clay moulds. The most recent method, however, is the making of wax moulds by centrifugal/investment casting.

Casting is used both to mass-produce components and to create limited edition pieces. But there is a distinct difference between costume jewelry made from mass-produced findings and that made from original, hand-crafted moulds. The use of findings – stamped tin or alloy components, such as chains sold by the metre, and stamped motifs for brooches, buttons, earrings and medallions and decorative filigrees – inevitably produces jewelry with a standardized appearance.

Another recent development which has changed not only the look but also the components of costume jewelry is the injection moulding of plastics. Many of the factories using this technique were originally involved in glass making, but as glass (and metal) became more expensive, the firms switched to plastics.

Many manufacturers in Rhode Island, USA, the production centre of American costume jewelry, use the techniques of centrifugal casting and injection moulding of plastics to specialize in mass-produced findings and popular costume jewelry which is not linked specifically to fashion collections but is marketed to complement a season's general look. The introduction of gold-plating techniques to the established fine jewelry industry in Rhode Island by Nehemiah Dodge in the late eighteenth century facilitated the development of a cheap jewelry industry. By the nineteenth century several firms based in Providence, Rhode Island, provided soldering, polishing and gilding techniques which were later employed by the costume jewelry industry. The subsequent rise of the five-and-dime store and the escalating demand for cheap jewelry by the turn of the century prompted further mechanical improvements, such as drop presses and chain-mesh-producing and screw machines which were used by both jewelers

Left Schiaparelli's red drap evening jacket fastened with peanut-shaped buttons, 1935. *Christian Bérard*

Below Elsa Schiaparelli, wearing a massive diamanté collier and cuff which echo the thick embroidery on her white wool evening jacket, 1941. *Horst P. Horst*

and findings companies. By the 1920s the requirements for costume jewelry production in Rhode Island could be satisfied for two reasons: first, the indigenous skills and machines that had developed in the fine jewelry industry; and, second, the labour pool of Portuguese immigrants who had settled there, originally to fish the Gulf Stream waters, but later to take up the intricate handwork of jewelry production. Since the Second World War, capital-intensive, high-technology methods of production, such as mechanized polishing tubs and gilding baths, have gradually replaced labour intensive methods.

The Rhode Island companies supply components or made-up pieces to the many small costume jewelry wholesalers and designers centred between 37th and 39th Streets in New York City. Here, every other shop window twinkles with assorted sequins, beads, beaded fringes, tin findings spilling out of wicker baskets or cardboard boxes, like an Aladdin's cave of pantomime gewgaws. These components, sold to costume jewelry designers around the city, are bought by the kilo or hundred. Occasionally an ethnic novelty, such as a soapstone buddha, Indian gilt filigree setting or a bag full of African painted wooden beads, sits invitingly in a window, inspiring a passer-by to use it as the centrepiece of a necklace or brooch.

By contrast, the craftsman approach still prevails in Paris. Around the Place de la République tiny Dickensian sweatshops create intricate and limited edition pieces for the grand couture houses. Some of the oldest findings companies can also be discovered in the troisième arrondissement. Janvier, for example, established in 1840 by M. Vennin and M. Peltier, and Dreyfus, established in 1886, supply the jewelry industry with an extensive and growing archive (now over 150,000 models) of chains, links, clips, earring backs and stampings which are constantly incorporated into jewelry design.

By 1869 twenty-eight of these companies, centred in Le Marais, rue Charlot, rue des Gravillers, rue de Temple, rue des Archives, rue Pastourelle and rue des Vertus, had decided to unite under the 'Chambre Syndicale des Graveurs, Estampeurs et Apprêteurs' to protect their general interests. They set up an apprenticeship scheme and tried to copyright their designs. A law was passed recognizing and registering copyright in April 1938. The companies now export under the collective title Framex.

Outside Paris, the mountainous region of Oyonax in the south of France evolved as a supplier of horn for the combs, hair ornaments and trinket boxes used in the nineteenth and early twentieth centuries. As the indigenous herds of horned animals diminished and the supply became prohibitively expensive, a plastic industry developed, providing a substitute material. Today much of the plastic for jewelry and sunglasses comes from this area.

Above A selection of tin findings from the Framex Group of Manufacturers in Paris, 1987

Opposite Paloma Picasso, wearing her own jewelry with a Valentino dress, 1981. *Barry Lategan*

Far left An earring created from salvage of old keys suspended from a chain, 1984. *Albert Watson*

Left Dior's shoulder-length, chandelier paste earrings, 1949. *Horst P. Horst*

Japan, Korea, the United States, Britain, Italy, West Germany and Austria are the chief costume jewelry producers today – Birmingham; London; Milan; Pforzheim, Kaufbeuren and Neugablonz in West Germany and Enns in Austria being the major towns involved. In Kaufbeuren, jewelry is created in a way reminiscent of the traditional Czechoslovakian origins of the craft. Tiny chalets, painted with folkloric murals, house costume jewelry workshops in kitchen or basement. This antiquated cottage industry supplies hand-cut and -strung beads and rhinestone-pasted pieces.

Costume jewelry is one of the essential accessories that complete a couture or ready-to-wear collection. As with other accessories – hats, bags, belts, gloves, shoe ornaments and umbrellas – the emphasis which leading designers place upon it varies from season to season. Consequently, most of the established creators of accessories are united under and represented by the Chambre Syndicale des Paruriers which, like its fellow union, the Chambre Syndicale de la Couture, ensures that wages, working conditions and the economic security of the industry are controlled and that a collective voice can be heard by the fashion houses and government alike.

Costume jewelry has always given a clear reflection of fashion. Pick up a riotously coloured glass 'fruit salad' brooch – it immediately spells the late thirties; a chandelier paste earring – the late forties; huge plastic hoops and an aluminium breastplate – the mid-sixties; a fey, rustic, enamel butterfly pendant – the early seventies; a swag of 'creative salvage' (buttons, bottle tops, bones, crosses) – the eighties. Its throwaway nature liberates both designers and customers to keep up with the prevailing style in fashion. Its intrinsic worthlessness casts it as an outsider, a rôle that has always fostered daring, initiative and drama.

Opposite Paste-embedded resin 'rock' jewelry by Anne Fern for Fred Spurr, 1984. *Albert Watson*

1 · 1909 –1918

Tentative Beginnings: Dress Garniture and Accessories

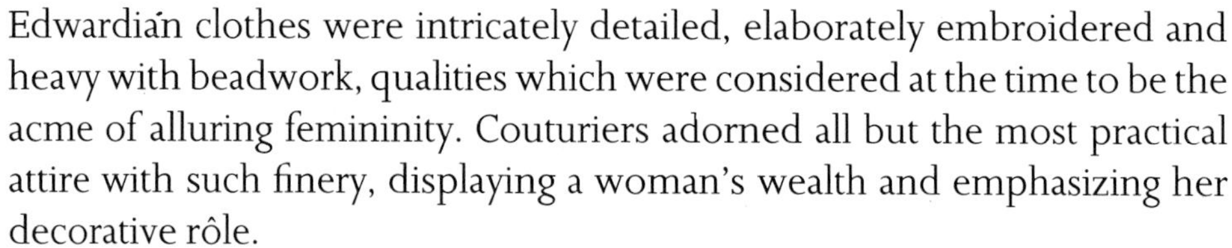

Edwardian clothes were intricately detailed, elaborately embroidered and heavy with beadwork, qualities which were considered at the time to be the acme of alluring femininity. Couturiers adorned all but the most practical attire with such finery, displaying a woman's wealth and emphasizing her decorative rôle.

Formal gowns were weighted down with stone- and sequin-sewn decorations, known as garnitures. These included detachable net or lace panels in the form of fichus which were wrapped about the throat; deep, decorative collars, known as berthas; or bretelles (braces) which glistened with applied beadwork. Signifying even greater formality and luxury, evening dresses were entirely covered with beadwork. Bugle beads, pearls, cabochons, steel beads, nail heads, rhinestones and jet, some as small as pin heads, others as large as coins, twinkled in the candlelight. Wraps, shawls and capes fringed with crystal, tinsel, paillettes and porcelain beads were drawn about the shoulders as women stepped out into the night.

Those who could not afford to be dressed by the grand couturiers could buy bejewelled and beaded garnitures from department stores to ornament and update an evening gown or blouse. Bead-decorated net or Brussels lace pieces were priced according to workmanship. Of varying lengths, they could be slipped over a dress, some just clearing the floor, for dancing, others merely covering the bodice.

Alternatively, a bead-decorated net, chiffon or muslin scarf could be wrapped across the shoulders, or a cabochon-strung bertha or bolero could enhance the neck, shoulders and chest of an evening ensemble. Single ornaments, such as a butterfly- or flower-shaped rhinestone motif, or a beaded girdle, could be bought by the piece or the yard and sewn to the bodice or waist of a gown.

Trinkets, ornate pins, haircombs and shoe buckles added further elaboration to a toilette. Chiffon or lace fichus were held in place with fine stick pins, brooches, buttons and buckles, and *Vogue* emphasized that these details were 'important out of all proportion to their size'. Virtually every

Above Beaded net butterfly ornament and oval belt buckle of pearl beads outlined by double lines of rhinestones and clear glass beads, 1913

Opposite White and silver satin evening dress with an elaborate bodice of pearl and white brilliants, and occasional tassels of iridescent pearls and crystal beads on a net veil. Pearl and stone chandelier earrings echo the dress garniture, 1918. *Baron Adolphe de Meyer*

Selection of pearl and brilliants-encrusted buckles, 1916

woman scooped her hair on top of her head with rhinestone-set, tortoise-shell hairpins and celluloid combs, beneath hats secured with crystal, ebony and onyx hatpins.

Even the plainest of day shoes was decorated with a steel buckle, while evening shoes glistened with marcasite and cut-stone-decorated ornaments. Diana Vreeland recalls her knee-high observation of the fashionable women in Paris 'walking through the Bois with tiny, mincing steps .... Their shoes were so beautiful! Children, naturally, are terribly aware of feet. They're closer to them. I remember shoe buckles of eighteenth-century paste, which is so much more beautifully cut than rhinestones are – so much richer looking. I love décor on the foot.' By 1913 *Vogue* had impressed upon its readers that for too long they had been satisfied with either simple English or 'home made' shoes and must now realize that ornate shoe buckles were *de rigueur* for an elegant foot. A rhinestone or chased and etched enamel buckle could be bought to finish off the vamp of a slipper or a coloured glass buckle could be held in place by a ribbon on the instep.

A hat's character was defined by the originality of its decoration, so milliners along the rue de la Paix were indebted to the artfulness of their trinket suppliers. Strings of fabulously decorative beads were wrapped around a crown; a pin held a precarious balance of felt, straw or fur; or a grosgrain band was adorned with a pretty buckle or aigrette.

Companies were set up around the couture quarter of Paris which imported imitation pearls and strass from Bohemia and Germany to supply the couturiers and accessory makers with trinkets or their components. Fried Frères had been established by the eponymous brothers, Gustave and Otto, in the rue de la Caire in 1886. By 1918, their sons, Jean and Lucien, had branched out to become principal suppliers of findings, stones and costume jewelry to the major department stores. The Paris company of Fath, Magone and Hobé specialized in 'bugle gowns' for the theatre which were decorated with tiny beads and sequins. Florenz Ziegfeld (of the Ziegfeld Follies) was one of their most important customers. From the mid-twenties these firms, and others such as Lyon Weill, a major competitor, offered costume jewelry – a service that developed into a thriving business.

Above Purple velvet poke bonnet, trimmed with purple grosgrain ribbon embroidered in crystal and gold beads, 1917

Right Scarabs, locusts and other insect shapes cast in matt metals were popular with the Edwardians for buckles and buttons, 1909

Pforzheim in West Germany had been a centre of fine jewelry-making since the eighteenth century and had become the major centre of production in Europe. The tradition had originated when a local duke who ran an orphanage occupied the children by teaching them jewelry-making skills. By the beginning of the twentieth century some companies in the town began creating fashion and hair accessories. Florien Grossé and his brother-in-law, Heinrich Henkel, for example, originally specialized in making haircombs trimmed with gold, but, as the demand developed, branched out after the war into costume jewelry. Similarly, Coro (later known as Corocraft), established in the United States in 1906 by Cohn & Rosenberger; Napier Incorporated, America's oldest fashion jewelry house, founded in 1875; and Gustav Trifari, Carl Fischel and Leo Krussman, who worked for Rice & Hochster in New York, all made haircombs, shoe buckles, handbag clasps and liberty pins (to hold the straps of the numerous articles of lingerie in place) for the fashionable market.

Strawberry-shaped pendant set with seed pearls, 1917

During the opening years of the century, the main purpose of semi- and non-precious jewelry was imitation. It was not true costume jewelry. Foil-backed glass mimicked rubies and emeralds, vulcanized rubber simulated jet, marcasite posed as diamonds and glass beads as pearls. Imitation was acceptable, frank fakery for decorative effect was not.

Fashionable women were consequently hesitant to wear non-precious jewelry. However, three factors gradually broke down its stigma: the effect of the Art Nouveau movement, which highlighted the aesthetic rather than the monetary value of materials; repeated editorial promotion; and couture sanctioning of imitation and non-precious jewelry as an addition, not an alternative, to fine jewelry.

Relatively valueless materials, such as coral, amber, seed pearls and jet, were enjoyed for their decorative effect rather than their intrinsic value and were worn with the same nonchalant air with which one would wear plastic or gilt today. The Western market was flooded with Hungarian jewelry, made from silver enamel and very poor stones (such as pale coloured, 'white' emeralds lifted with green foil), and popularly styled in the manner of ornamental Renaissance jewelry. St George and the dragon motifs and flora and fauna figures were also popular.

A selection of pearl, garnet and lapis lazuli Hungarian jewelry, 1913

Numerous dealers in semi-precious jewelry and trinkets tried to satisfy a growing market. Don McDonald, a travelling salesman for Walter Scaife Ltd, founded in London in 1915, recalls the exhausting and humiliating task of carrying his tray of pins and baubles round the major department stores and cobblers. Having waited endlessly in a row of rival salesmen, the chief buyer would march up the line pointing at 'You, you, you and you', and the rest had to pack up and go, dismissed.

Dress garniture was sewn either directly on to gowns or on to embellished, attachable ornaments, berthas and bretelles. Several hundred hours of handiwork went into making a heavily beaded gown; hand-dyed beads and sequins or cut-glass stones were individually sewn or glued on to the material.

Opposite page, above Agate dress garniture mounted in a cup-shaped socket of dull gilt, 1911

Far left Tarnished green ormolu (gilt bronze) garniture set composed of Mercury wings, a plaited *cocarde* on the fur hat and matching *passementerie* swags closing the neck-piece and stole, 1909

Centre Décolleté garniture of opalescent bugles, 1909

Below Bolero of jet cabochons and bugles, 1909

This page Buzenet's black net evening dress spangled with jet, with diamanté sleeve clasps, 1909. *Felix*

Left Black satin slipper with high Louis heel, piped in white satin, laced with black and white cothurn ribbon and jewelled with rhinestones, 1913

Below left Jet and rhinestone buckle, 1913

Below centre Decorative afternoon shoe in white leather, bronze kid and patent leather trim with a dull bronze and jet buckle, 1914

Below right Court shoe rimmed in rhinestones with high, brilliant-studded heel, 1913

Opposite Selection of chased, etched and enamel buckles from The Gorham Company, New York, for dresses, shoes and veil pins, 1909

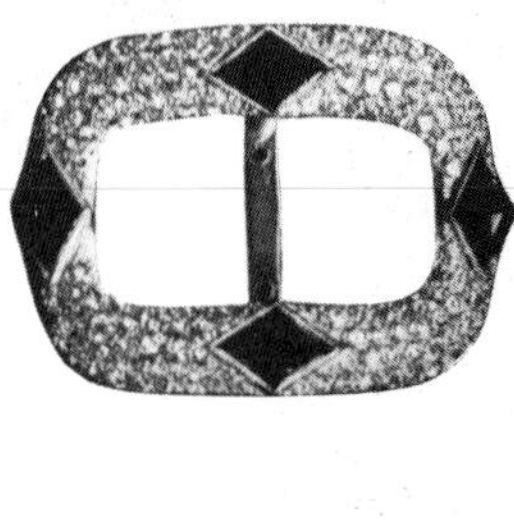

Shoe buckles and shoe ornaments became indispensable accessories as feet emerged from the dark ages of Victorianism where they had been hidden under layers of long skirts and petticoats. Inevitably, as hemlines began to rise, the small, well-shod foot became a decorative focal point, and by 1910 buckled shoes were ubiquitous. As the decade progressed, large flat buckles were ousted by tinier, ever more decorative buckles.

Black or tan shoes, worn by day, were not generally ornamented, although fancy-topped afternoon shoes could sport flat mother-of-pearl or bone buttons. A variety of coloured slippers in various sumptuous materials were worn for the evening but black satin or black patent were considered to be the most serviceable. A cut-steel, rhinestone, silver or jet buckle or ornament was *de rigueur*, combined with modest little rhinestone buttons set in a ribbon or a chiffon rosette. For shoes of bronze kid, *Vogue* recommended gilt slides or buckles. On grand occasions, slippers matched the gown's material, decorated with coloured stone buckles, spangled embroidery, hand painting or tulle rosettes. Buckle sets could be bought separately and attached, to add variety. The shapes of the buckles and the shapes of the stones set in them changed from season to season, the most usual being oval, square or round.

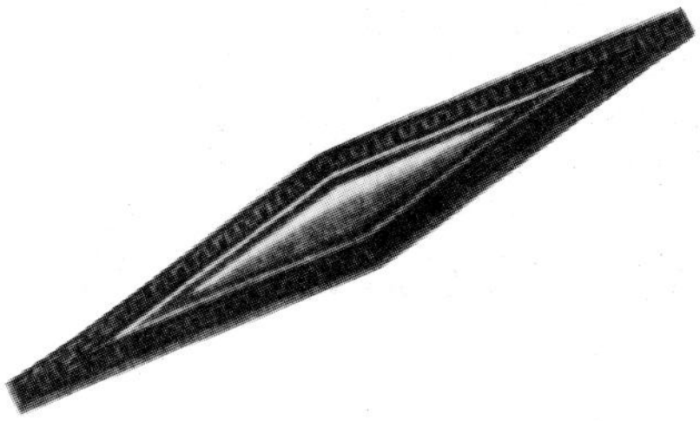

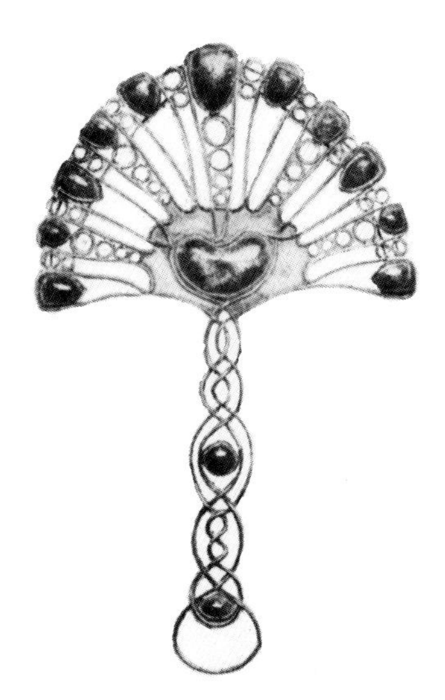

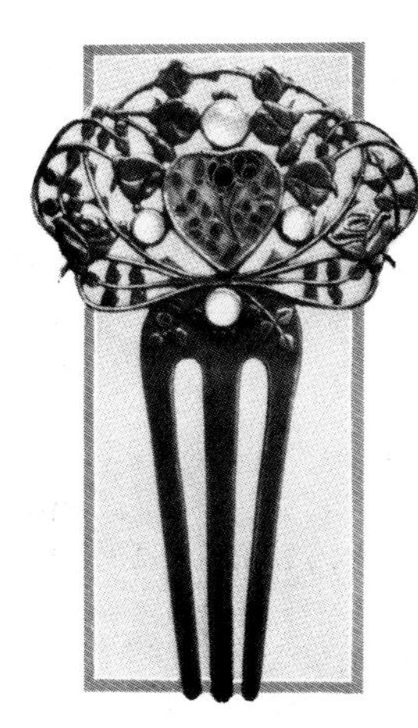

Far left Beaten silver and enamel Art Nouveau fan-holder, 1917

Left Miss Strange's Art Nouveau pink and green enamel comb set with opal and chrysoprase stones, 1914

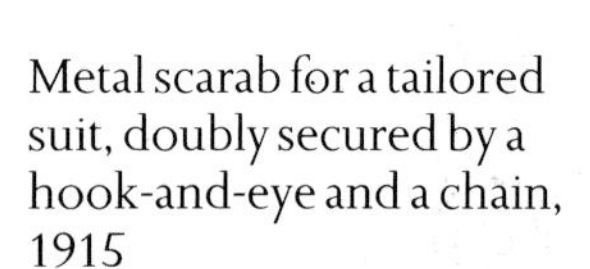

Metal scarab for a tailored suit, doubly secured by a hook-and-eye and a chain, 1915

Grades of trinket jewelry were sharply differentiated. The setting of paste or strass, for example, was inferior to marcasite. While marcasite was cut like regular, tiny crystals and set into claws – as one would set a fine gem – paste was foiled and set into an already stamped setting – no claws were used. Marcasite tended to be set in silver, paste in base metal. Black dots, painted on the base of each of the smaller stones to increase the appearance of depth, were used to enhance paste as well as real diamonds. Even the fine jewelry houses, such as Cartier, offered marcasite novelty pins and brooches.

Imitation pearls were also particularly popular in this period. Egyptian themes, such as scarabs, locusts and other insects (many derivative of the Art Nouveau movement) made of base metal, cabochon turquoises, coloured crystals and tiger's eyes, were sported on buttons and buckles. *Vogue* singled out the Arts and Crafts parures to be worn with tailor-mades for their appropriate and decorative effect.

The jewelry historian Vivienne Becker considered jewelry to be 'the most intense expression of the Art Nouveau movement' and observed that it was the renewed interest in the decorative arts that encouraged many artists to turn their hand to this medium. Both the Art Nouveau and Arts and Crafts movements reacted against mass-produced Victorian jewelry. The aesthetic qualities of 'natural' materials – the patina of stones, the colours of *pâte de verre* and enamel or the subdued tones of horn – began to be appreciated, and contemporary taste was gradually weaned away from the unimaginatively ostentatious towards the visually pleasing.

Enamel jewelry, be it *plique à jour* or *cloisonné*, was typical of the Art Nouveau mode and was a particularly popular means of matching the colour of jewelry to the colour of an outfit. By 1909 *Vogue* had observed, 'Everywhere enamel; it is the basis of trinkets and accessories of various kinds,... It finishes off a toilet most delightfully, as any colour scheme of the costume may be carried out with it, and whether combined with precious stones or set off merely by a background of gold or silver, it is unfailingly attractive. Pendants are its most popular form.'

In the same year *Vogue* began to assure its readers that semi-precious or imitation pins or ornaments were gaining acceptance among well-dressed women 'who realise the inappropriateness of gems for simple frocks and tailored gowns.... Semi-precious and imitation jewelry of a certain kind, if of refined style and correctly displayed, may be worn with very smart effect. The pieces, however, must be most judiciously selected, and displayed with the greatest discretion.' A high-society woman might, therefore, consider wearing a novelty pin on her golfing outfit or walking suit, but would be wary of donning anything but formal, fine jewelry for evening wear.

Vogue's initial reaction to costume, rather than semi-precious, jewelry was circumspect, partly reflecting high society's scepticism about its acceptability and partly due to the magazine's dependence on advertising revenue from the fine jewelry houses. Indeed, before the war, *Vogue* regarded the ateliers producing semi-precious or costume jewelry as rather quaint, if not quirky. Under such headings as 'Little drops of semi-precious stones and little grains of enamel go to making craftsman jewelry,' American *Vogue* in 1914 reported on the Englishwoman, Miss Strange, in Washington, who 'works at long narrow benches spread with innumerable bits of coloured enamel, silver, gold, precious and semi-precious stones and with skilful and swift hands fashions the most artistic and ornamental types of jewelry.' She was particularly proficient at *plique à jour* enamelling which she used for jewelry and coat and cape buttons. In commending her work, the writer observed that the monetary value of such stones and settings was secondary to the 'decorative merit of their colour.' Similarly in Florence in 1910 an enterprising American, Mrs Arthur Murray Cobb, was producing 'artistic jewelry' in leather, brass and copper, most of which was antique-finished. However, despite the editorial coverage in *Vogue*, the work of these women was still regarded as peripheral to high fashion. It took the sanction of the *grandes maisons* to encourage its general acceptance.

Mrs Arthur Murray Cobb's Gothic-style collar of dull silver plaques and square-cut amethysts, 1910

The rigid sartorial etiquette of the time, which costume jewelry was attempting to subvert, was exemplified in the wearing of mourning jewelry. Following Queen Victoria's precise lead, women were expected to encase themselves in black for at least a year, displaying both wealth and decorum. Black bombazine or crêpe upholstered bosoms were pinned and hung with carved brooches, pendants and lockets of Whitby jet. The latter, a fossilized wood washed up on the shores of the Yorkshire seaside town, was immensely popular, so much so that demand soon outstripped supply, and alternatives, such as *bois dulci*, vulcanite and French jet, inevitably made their appearance.

Hat pins and ornaments assumed great importance in the early years of this century. Fashionable milliners vied with each other not only to create the most eye-catching swathes, or balances of material, on the heads of their clients but also to trim these with ornate garnitures, pins and novelties.

Above Turbans – promoted by Poiret – were highly fashionable in 1909. Carlier's bombe-shaped, voluminous crown of rose-coloured, draped velvet is twisted with two other velvets of lighter tones and interlaced with a string of mauve and silver metal beads that nestle in the folds of the velvet

Right Carlier drapes deep black velvet over the turban base. In the centre the material ends are loosely knotted, bandanna fashion, producing 'rabbit ear' effects at each side. The folds are held in place by a large hammered metal ornament, 1909

Opposite page, above left Cabochon pearls set in a rhinestone base decorate the tops of veil and hat pins, 1911

Below left Grey and beige swathed crêpe-de-Chine toque crowned with beige satin quills and encircled with large, opaque, dull gold beads, 1918

Top According to *Vogue*, the over-ornate hatpin was *outré*. It recommended instead this selection of simple pins, 1910

Above Rénard's black tulle-draped, bowl-shaped hat. The base of the crown is encircled by a wide girdle of large, polished jet beads, finished off at the side of the head with a large cabochon-cut jet ornament, 1909

Right Wartime motoring hat of grey felt stitched in grey. A bold jet buckle decorates the brim, 1917

Left Selection of hair ornaments. *Bottom* barrette of demi-blond shell and rhinestone; *left to right* aluminium and rhinestone pin; comb with real shell rim around an amber centre; crystal-encrusted pin; feather pin of aluminium and rhinestone, 1914

Below Selection of jewelled hairpins from Altmans, New York, used to catch a veil close to the hair at the sides of a coiffure, 1913

Opposite page, above left A highly decorative rhinestone comb, 1914

Centre Rice & Hochster's platinum-finished metal-and-rhinestone comb, 1914

Far right Demi-blond shell pin with a rhinestone-studded top, 1915

Below left Cut-jet back comb, 1909

Below centre Strass-set amber haircombs, 1913

Below right Two-pronged, demi-amber braid pin, 1917

Hair ornaments decorated the spectacular coiffure that was an Edwardian woman's crowning glory. The hair was swept up, for height was *de rigueur*, and rolled to the front of the head to bare the nape of the neck, while covering the ears. Pins of plain shell were preferred by day, while an evening toilette was set aglitter with rhinestone- or paste-set combs.

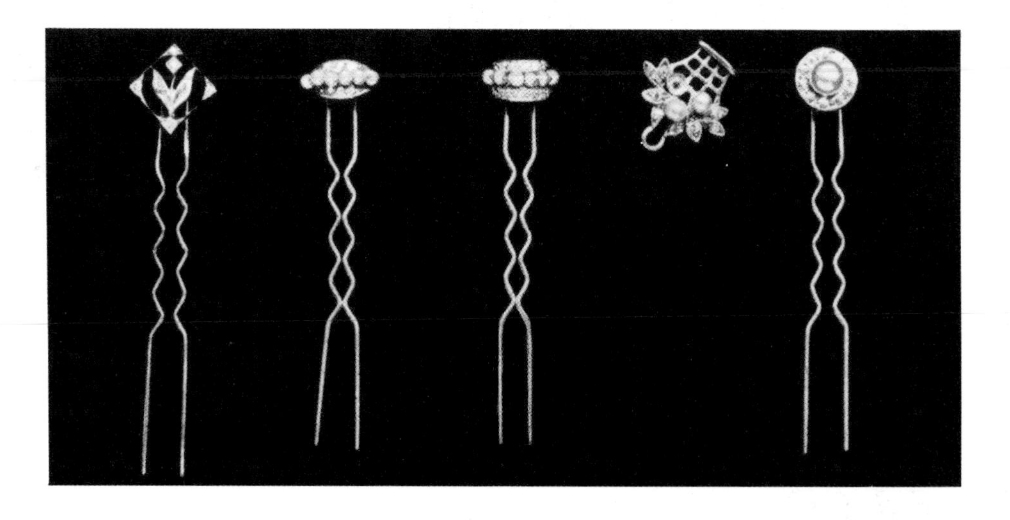

The change from the elaborate ornamentation associated with Edwardiana to the more functional Modernist style was clearly reflected in fashionable clothing and jewelry. Jewelers began paring down the decorative details on avant-garde pieces. In tracing the birth of Modernism, it is essential to look at the work of the Danish silversmith Georg Jensen. Although he was not a costume jeweler, his work reflected the direction that contemporary design, including dress, was to take. His clean lines and appreciation of the intrinsic, unembellished qualities of the materials he worked in, notably sterling silver, influenced fine and costume jewelry alike. Jensen's audience grew when a shop displaying his work opened in Berlin in 1909. His sculptural simplicity and bold abstraction were to become Modernist traits repeated throughout the century. Similar styles were revived by Elsa Peretti and Paloma Picasso for Tiffany's in the 1970s and by Robert Lee Morris of Artwear for Donna Karan in the 1980s.

Hand-painted and block-printed buttons from Poiret's Martine School, 1913

Like Jensen, the new aesthetics associated with Serge Diaghilev's Ballets Russes and then introduced into the fashion world by Paul Poiret, in the form of clean-cut, Eastern-influenced silhouettes decorated in blocks of bold colour, guided contemporary taste away from elaborate ornamentation towards sharply defined form emphasized by vivid colour. Poiret had experimented with costume jewelry while training at the house of Doucet, and he was the first couturier to consider using it in his collection. Commissioning the Parisian jewelers René Boivin and Gripoix, and the artist Paul Iribe, he accessorized his clothes with tassel-style jewelry. His blue brocade evening dress of 1912, for instance, was trimmed with a drawstring, silk tasselled sash and matching beaded and tasselled pendant, while another from the same collection was decorated with a silver, tasselled pendant hung with steel cube-shaped and glass beads and a metal buddha. Similarly, Paul Iribe designed a pair of tassels consisting of an amethyst cap and a long fringe of oblong pearls suspended on silk cords round the neck of a 1913 Poiret outfit, entitled 'Nocturne'. Gripoix and his wife made *pâte de verre* jewelry for Poiret and created a glass aquarium filled with real and glass fish for his salon.

By 1913 Poiret-style pendants hanging from coloured cords were offered in department stores on both sides of the Atlantic. They included amber hearts, vegetable-dye-coloured beads and stone buddhas which complemented the Eastern mode of dress.

Poiret worked closely with the fine jeweler René Boivin, as costume jewelry made at the beginning of the century largely depended upon labour-intensive, fine jewelry-making techniques, in contrast to the more 'efficient', though less intricate, methods used today. Labour was cheap. Donald Hobé of Hobé Cie explained that the cost of labour at the beginning

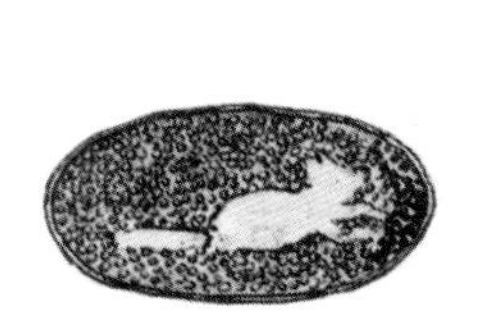

of the century was never more than 10 percent of the finished item. Consequently, laborious methods of production could be afforded, such as hand-setting glass in claws, rather than using glue, or hand-painting – practices which have become virtually obsolete today because of prohibitive costs.

By the eve of the First World War the intricate, delicate and 'pretty' jewelry styles of the Edwardian years had been entirely replaced by large, simpler pieces; Modernism had prevailed. Even the size of jewelry boxes had to be reconsidered, as Anne Fogarty pointed out in her book *The Art of Being a Well-Dressed Woman* (1913): 'Baubles too must breathe. Crushed together, they lose their vigour. Their lustre fades or is scratched. With the profusion and size of costume jewelry today, the ordinary jewel box may not be adequate. A neighbour of ours uses an old-fashioned sewing box that has an enormous, plush-lined section which she uses for chunky bracelets and necklaces, and a dozen drawers formerly holding spools of thread now contain beads, earrings, and pins.'

During the war, interest in precious jewelry waned. *Vogue* considered it to be entirely appropriate that 'with the reduction of living to its simplest terms, jewels, like the costume, are marked by a new simplicity. The more ornate forms have given way to the clear cut designs, plain almost to severity but full of new significance.' As it became vulgar and inappropriate to wear expensive jewelry, so alternative decoration was sought. Many turned to trinkets to lift a gown at a fund-raising ball, and in 1916 *Vogue* reported: 'All that glitters is not gold, or all scintillating stones diamonds, but a pretty design and a sparkling effect may be obtained for £2.19s.6d.'

In Germany, women were encouraged to surrender their gems to the government to raise money for the war effort; in return, they were issued with Berlin iron jewelry. A precedent for this had been set during the War of Liberation (1813-15), when the Royal Berlin Factory issued Berlin iron jewelry for similar reasons. *Vogue* featured jewelry and trinkets – such as brooches and pins – made by recuperating Allied soldiers, in copper, tin, zinc and even shrapnel. 'This year [1916] a hat shows patriotism by wearing a metal ornament made by a wounded soldier of France.' Many fashionable Parisian milliners were featuring on their hats trimmings made by soldiers. Jingoistic costume jewelry, such as aviator's wings, regimental badges and victory flags, accompanied the masculine and pseudo-military styles of dress adopted by women.

Above left Wounded soldiers in France made the bead and worsted embroidery ornament (left) and the tin and bright stone ornament (right), 1916

Above Dull yellow and steel necklace of flat beads, made by a wounded soldier, 1917

Below Diamanté arrow pin from Dreicer, 1918

Delicate artificial and seed-pearls were a perfect complement to the pale, sweet-pea-coloured Edwardian clothes. Similarly, the dramatic contrast of black and white, so popular during the war, was well served by large, iridescent pearls.

Opposite Pearl-strung Juliet cap formed by strands of evenly sized beads strung on a fine gold wire. Large baroque plaques of dark blue, peacock blue, green and grey-pink enamelled metal are set between rows of pearls which droop over the temples, 1909

Above Reville created a striking contrast of black and white for the older woman: a black tabard over a white crêpe full-sleeved blouse decorated with rows of tiny pearls from the elbow to the wrist. Ropes of pearls hang down the front, 1917

Above right Black velvet, pearl-edged head-dress, 1911

Right Pearls looped from the high Russian head-dress and strung across the *décolleté* make a tier from throat to waist, 1916

Jet and mourning jewelry abided by the strict social codes of Edwardian mourning, originally set by Queen Victoria. 'The little things of mourning must be chosen with great care and should never depart from the plainest kind of treatment,' said *Vogue* in 1911. Simple, undecorated religious symbols and sentimental mementos satisfied these codes.

Left Doeuillet's slim evening gown with a jet-embroidered corsage and front panel, suspended from long jet shoulder straps, and ending in a jet tassel which delineates the train, 1917

Above Five-piece gun-metal chatelaine, consisting of an oval mirror, a memo pad, a powder box, a smelling-salts bottle and a tortoise-shell comb hinged like a penknife into a case, 1911

Right Intricately carved necklace with hanging pendants of Whitby jet – a reproduction of an antique design, 1909

Below right Cut-jet necklace and simple Whitby jet cross

Opposite Selection of mourning jewelry – a jet cross, jet oval brooch, and thin black velvet ribbons worn round the wrist and waist, 1918. *Helen Dryden*

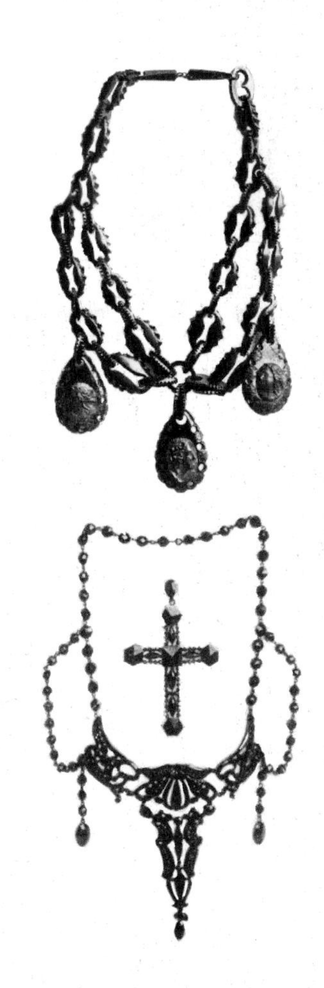

Enamel 'Blighty' charm, 1916

Many jewelry factories turned to the production of arms and munitions to aid the war effort, as their precision equipment and craftsmanship could easily be transferred to ammunition and gun part manufacturing. The Americans made this shift very smoothly. The jewelry trade had flourished there from 1900 to the war. But with the halting of imports during hostilities – and in particular the loss of imitation stones from Germany and Austria, the industry was left short of components.

Gradually the exigencies of war affected the mode of dress and by 1918 *Vogue* reported that restraint prevailed in most circles: 'With the adoption of a more conservative standard of dress, which seems to be the smart woman's solution to the war problem as applied to her clothes, the importance of accessories of the costume has become even more strongly emphasized.... very prominent among these accessories is the string of pearls... it is possible to imitate pearls quite perfectly, and one may purchase a really lovely imitation strand without paying a large sum.'

It was not until after the First World War that seasonal costume jewelry finally came into its own. That it did so was entirely due to the sartorial confidence of two women – Gabrielle Chanel and Elsa Schiaparelli. Their determination to add humour and variety to costume jewelry further removed it from cautious imitation and stamped it with its most engaging characteristics – stylishness, nonchalant luxury and wit.

Left Pink quilted satin mules decorated with braid and rosettes; a green-gold novelty link chain with a square filigree locket, set with a black and white cameo and artificial pearls, 1918

Opposite Lavishly embroidered Russian blouse of café-au-lait net, finished with a fringe of crocheted beads and worn with a heavy bead necklace with a stone and crystal pendant, 1918. *Baron Adolphe de Meyer*

Tassels, according to Paul Poiret, were 'the tools of coquetry'. Many were decorated with oriental motifs, such as Buddhas and Chinese mandarins, to echo the Eastern-inspired lines of Poiret's clothes.

Left Tassels suspended from silken cords are the sole decoration on Poiret's minaret tunic dress entitled 'Nocturne', 1913. *Geisler and Baumann*

Below Poiret's tan cord, hung with an amber heart and green tassel and his long chain of green, pink and red vegetable beads and tiny steel beads, 1913

Opposite page, top left A chain of Chinese beads – red, black and gold – strung on a tan cord with a large jade bead as a central motif, 1913

Top right A rich tasselled girdle, hanging long and low, gives an exotic touch to the paisley dress and oriental beads by Reville, 1916

Below A pear-shaped jade ornament on a woven green cord, held in place by a Chinese mandarin emblem, and worn on a white muslin and lace blouse, 1918. *Charlotte Fairchild*

2 · 1919–1945

Chanel's 'Nonchalance de Luxe', Schiaparelli's Surrealism

Above Worth drapes swags of pearls over the arms of his model, creating a pseudo-sleeve, 1920

Below Chéruit wraps strings of beads round the waist of a simple shift, 1920

The social upheavals of the war had changed fashionable taste. It was now influenced by the *nouveaux riches*, who had benefitted from the redistribution of wealth and who thirsted for change. They promoted a taste for boldness, novelty and fun, deeming old-fashioned any historicism or restraint in design. It was no longer chic to parade inherited gems (few possessed them anyway); instead, large, highly 'designed', angular jewels were introduced, to complement the hard, straight, androgynous lines of clothing.

Immediately following the war, Paris ordained that the heavily beaded evening dress was *de rigueur*. Simple, sleeveless sack-dresses and later sheath-dresses lay heavily against the body, weighted with bugle beads, crystal baguettes and jet panels.

The different cut of clothes demanded new functions of jewelry. Muff chains, fichu pins and lockets gave way to four-foot-long strings of pearls, crystal and glass beads or *sautoirs* to accentuate long, lean lines; sleeveless evening dresses left arms uncovered to bear bangles. Beaded ropes girdled the hips of waistless dresses and strings of gold and silver coloured beads criss-crossed legs to fasten dancing slippers. By 1925 the leg had been daringly revealed and even the knees of stockings were embellished with bugle beads. Worth and Chéruit hung swags of beads from shoulders and *Vogue* suggested that vine leaves could be threaded through them for an evening's novelty. Entire sleeves or backs of gowns consisted of rows and rows of pearls, and detachable lace sleeves were strung with glass beads. The couturier Beer reinterpreted the rosary, using carved wooden beads to sling across a day dress, while in 1920 Chéruit designed what *Vogue* called 'an ideal gown for a chaperon', which was hung with noisy beads. The short coiffure ousted ornate haircombs in favour of bandeaux, shingle pins (which held hair in a neat *chignon* behind the head) and angular brooches, which fastened a dress at the nape of the neck. By the mid-twenties the ubiquitous cloche and small beret were ornamented with small novelty pins.

Right and above Black crêpe frock embroidered entirely in pearls, crystal and tiny mirrors, 1925

Above The Grand Duchess Marie of Russia designed the motifs on this Chanel dress, inspired by a necklace belonging to the Romanov family, 1925

Below The Marquise de Chambray wears Chanel's short-sleeved white frock with a long string of jet beads, 1920

Opposite Nancy Cunard wears primitive art. African glazed wooden bangles – of varying tone and texture – are stacked up each arm, 1927. *Man Ray*

Trinket and costume jewelry manufacturers were forced either to cater for the new styles or go out of business. In 1921, Karl Fischel, an employee of the American firm Rice & Hochster, returned from holiday in France with alarming news. Fashionable Parisian women had bobbed their hair, rendering haircombs obsolete, and had stopped wearing high-topped shoes, so that ornate buckles were now redundant. Fischel and two of his colleagues, Gustav Trifari and Leo Krussman, decided to form their own company under the trade name 'T.F.K.' to supply the new costume jewelry market. In 1925, on the advice of an advertising agent, they changed their name to 'Trifari', which was thought to have a Continental, and therefore more elegant, ring. Trifari was to become one of the largest costume jewelry manufacturers in the world.

Postwar dress was distinguished by swaying movement and rattling noise, echoing the epoch's frenetic activity. Armloads of ivory and ebony bangles clattered with every gesture; ropes of pearls and crystal beads clicked around bare necks and cut-away backs were hung with jangling rows of beads.

Although the stigma of fake attached to costume jewelry had been challenged by Poiret before the war, it took the efforts of two influential women to repudiate it. Both were leading clothes designers and arbiters of postwar taste: Gabrielle 'Coco' Chanel and her rival, Elsa Schiaparelli.

Chanel regarded jewelry as an adornment and ridiculed those who craved gems simply for their monetary worth; fake could be mixed with real, displaying a cavalier attitude to value – *nonchalance de luxe*. Of course, Chanel was in a position to be cavalier. Her relationship with the emigré Grand Duke Dimitri of Russia had proved very lucrative; he had introduced her to unrestrained luxury and showered her with the magnificent Romanov jewels. Wearing these with casual aplomb, she would lay one on top of the other like swags of gewgaws. (Some say the insurance premiums were so vast that she was forced to wear them at all times.) 'It does not matter if they are real', she assured her admirers, 'so long as they look like junk.'

Chanel introduced her *vrais bijoux en toc* (fake jewelry that looks real) in 1924. Her interpretation of ornate Russian jewelry – long, long ropes of gilt chains hung with baroque pearls and *pâte de verre* crosses – was taken up by many women. None of these early pieces is signed. Chanel was significant not because she invented costume jewelry but because she was the first couturier regularly to design and commission idiosyncratic pieces for her collections. She stamped her blatantly fake creations with a distinctive house style which evolved from season to season, and which was entirely independent of the work being presented by the major jewelry houses, such as Van Cleef & Arpels and Boucheron.

Hair ornaments and hair fashions echoed the ancient Greek, Roman and Egyptian-inspired ensembles of the period. Tresses were drawn up from the nape of the neck and decorated with a wreath or diadem.

Opposite page, above left Roman-style wreath of pale green silvered leaves of velvet with clusters of white translucent grapes, 1920

Above centre An empire-shaped diadem in diamanté, worn low across the forehead, 1920

Above right Poised in a high knotted coiffure, a large Spanish comb of black metal, 1919. *Baron Adolphe de Meyer*

Below An Egyptian profile is achieved with an elaborate head-dress of brown tulle with large bronze glass beads dangling at the front and sides of the hair, 1920. *Baron Adolphe de Meyer*

This page Elaborate evening mantilla comb, 1923. *Edouard Benito*

A selection of Belperron's jewelry for Herz, worn by Mme Max Ernst, 1935; a collier of massive topazes, which seem invisibly mounted, with matching cuff and clips. *Horst P. Horst*

Chanel flaunted the fake as a symbol of confidence. The war had made women shy away from precious jewelry, which had an unpleasant association with the unpatriotic, inappropriate frivolity of the wives of war profiteers. Chanel responded to the new, independent role of postwar woman, who no longer wanted to be judged according to the value of the marriage she had made, as indicated by the costliness of her gems. Indeed, many women were to remain unmarried because of the loss of nearly an entire generation of young men in the war. By wearing fake jewelry a women could cock a snook at being 'kept', and proclaim her independence with a sartorial gesture of defiance.

Following the pioneering success of Chanel's *bijoux fantasie*, most of the grand couture houses teamed up with jewelers or artisans to present ranges to accompany their collections. Henkel and Grossé, for example, were commissioned by the couture houses Lanvin and Schiaparelli in 1928. Mme Belperron, a freelance fine jewelry designer, recognized the beauty of uncut and unprecious stones, such as smoky quartz and onyx, and devoted the same craftsmanship and daring to these humble materials as to the finest gems. Her influence in both fine and costume jewelry was far-reaching.

But the design of costume jewelry was not only affected by the biannual fashion changes. It also reflected movements in contemporary art. Ethnic sources, introduced to the fashionable world by the paintings and sculpture of Picasso, Brancusi, Arp, Modigliani and Gauguin, were reinterpreted by fashion and costume jewelry designers. Nancy Cunard's armloads of African ivories mirrored the contemporary taste for the ethnic, while bold galalith slave bangles decorated many bohemian wrists.

Numerous artists, including Picasso, Ernst, Man Ray, Derain, Braque, Arp and Calder, experimented with the jewelry medium, bringing novel shapes and materials to the field. Calder, for instance, made primitive jewelry for his friends out of coiled brass, silver or gold wire. Artists' ideas were occasionally incorporated into mass market pieces by manufacturers.

The aesthetic influence of Egyptology re-emerged following the discovery in 1922 of Tutankhamun's tomb and provoked a flood of imitative, Egyptian-style jewelry, such as scarab and 'Ba' bird pendants, necklaces and earrings. This theme was to remain popular for over a decade, further encouraged by Cecil B. de Mille's *Cleopatra* (1934).

In contrast to the splendid colours promoted by the fascination with Egyptology, the ubiquitous presence from 1914 onward of black and white in clothing and accessories reflected and served the dramatic contrasts of black and white photography which had entered the cultural life of the epoch. Designers played with transparent and opaque materials which reflected light, juxtaposing, for example, onyx and crystal glass beads.

Opposite *Vrais bijoux en toc*: pearl ropes, pear-shaped pendant earrings, cuffs heavy with diamanté and a Celtic-style gilt-and-paste pin, 1924. *Harriet Meserole*

OVERLEAF

Left Angular, leaf-shaped diamanté brooch, pinned to a cloche and worn with imitation pearls, 1927. *Georges Lepape*

Right Pearl, silver, jet and monogrammed enamel jewelry, featuring large stones in simple settings, 1926. *Edouard Benito*

BE
NI
TO

Crystal beads had become very fashionable and were in abundant supply, thanks to rich rock-crystal deposits which had been found before the war under Mount Kimbu, northwest of Mount Fuji, in the Yamanashi prefecture of Japan. Other black and white materials including enamels, ebony, ivory, onyx, marcasite and black and clear-coloured glass led *Vogue* to report in 1923 that 'the mode has a passion for black and white jewelry, particularly when the black is onyx and the white is marcasite.' One Chanel gimmick was to wear a white pearl in one ear and a black in the other.

Above O'Rossen's marcasite and silver animal clip, 1925

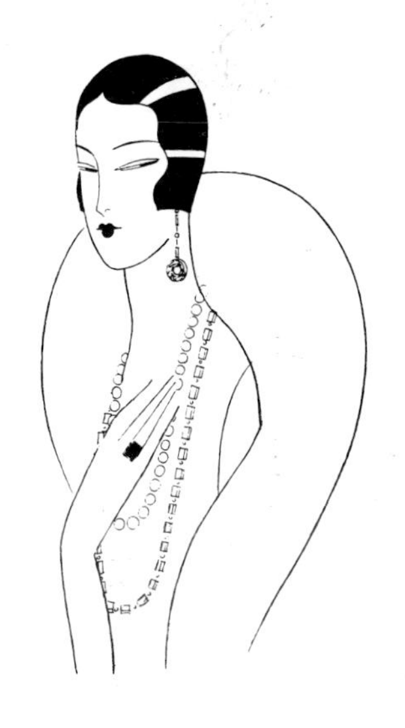

Below The ideal look for 1924: short Eton crop coiffure, Eastern-style make-up, and jade and cut-glass ropes of jewelry

Progress in aviation in the first quarter of the century was inevitably reflected in fashionable clothing, just as the space race influenced clothing in the sixties. Milliners, in particular, delighted in aviator helmet shapes, notably Poiret's milliner Madeleine Parizon, and for evening wear fringes of jet or pearl were hung from helmet-like head-dresses in imitation of earflaps. Speed and travel in general were recurrent themes in costume jewelry; the speed of the gazelle and greyhound, cars, trains, aeroplanes and ocean liners.

Finger rings became larger and larger, and the introduction of the cocktail brought with it the large-stoned, ornamental cocktail ring, which was all the rage among fashionable young women. The casual wearing of rings reflected a significant relaxation in the status codes of jewelry. Prior to the war it would have been considered inappropriate for a young, unmarried woman to flaunt any but the most modest of family rings; only mature leaders of society bedecked themselves with eye-catching decoration. However, by the mid-twenties every flapper announced her freedom by wearing sparkling rings how and where she chose.

During this period there had been an industrial breakthrough in the mass production of rings when lost-wax casting was supplemented by investment casting using liquid slurry (a technique originally invented for dental work). This eliminated metal shrinkage during casting. A further breakthrough by Jungersen in 1935 enabled metal wax patterns of complex structures to be cast at the same time. Pretty but inexpensive rings, such as rhinestones set in sterling silver, could now be bought at any department store to lift a sporty tweed suit or complement a shimmering cocktail dress.

The influence of Bauhaus functionalism in architecture and the applied arts in general dominated contemporary design. There was a new delight in machine-produced aesthetics; clearcut form replaced ornate detail. White, clear and diamond-like stones set into white metal, imitating platinum, were highly favoured, as were coloured combinations. Stones were cut in strict, geometrical shapes, typified by the *calibré* technique or elongated baguette. Many examples of these were exhibited at the Exposition des Arts Décoratifs in Paris in 1925.

Opposite 'Hat pins are back again,' reported *Vogue* in 1938. On a silk cushion a selection of jewelled pins to anchor and decorate the new, wide-brimmed hats. *Anton Bruehl*

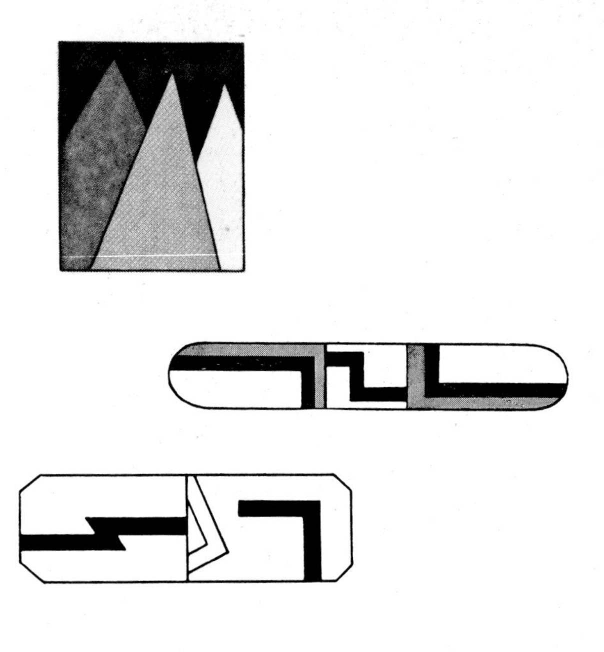

Above left Cloche hat pinned with an Art Deco brooch to match the brooch on the dress, 1927. *Maurice Beck and Helen Macgregor*

Above right Agnès's iceberg motif Art Deco ornament; Chanel's oxidized gold and silver belt buckle; Greidenberg's oxidized gold and silver buckle with Cubist-inspired motif. All 1925

Art Deco brooches were pinned on hats, waistbands and *décolletés*, or used to fix a fluttering Isadora-Duncan-style scarf to the shoulder. Gilded metal, oxidized or enamelled in blocks of colour, or marcasite set into silver were the most common variations offered by Greidenberg, Chanel, O'Rossen, Vevier and Paul Piel. Many fine jewelers, such as Raymond Templier, Georges Fouquet and Boucheron also turned their hands to these humbler materials. The Parisian milliner Agnès offered a range of Art Deco hatpins and many jewelers and fashion houses stocked plain or brilliants-encrusted metal, wood or enamelled belt buckles. Clips were attached to the edge of a *décolleté* or to the breast pocket of a suit and brightly beaded *sautoirs* encircled the neck. Highly coloured onyx, jade, turquoise or crystal *sautoirs* and pendants in Chinese or Egyptian style were suspended from black silken cords to lie against the popular black evening dresses of the early twenties. Now every aspect of a woman's attire could sport a piece of costume jewelry. By 1928, when the rage for beach attire had swept through fashionable resorts, the clothes designer Mary Nowitzky was even producing beach jewelry collections made of coloured shells.

Costume jewelry was an essential ingredient of Chanel's look, and she loved its permutations. Loth to sit unoccupied, even in conversation, she would perch in front of a tray, pushing glass stones into soft putty, arranging and rearranging the patterns. (One Parisian couturier keeps in his studio for inspiration a putty cast that was worked by Chanel.) Although many of the ideas were her own, Chanel also collaborated with Gripoix and Count Etienne de Beaumont. The husband-and-wife team, Gripoix, who had been commissioned by Poiret, updated Chanel's jewelry to accompany each season's clothes. The couple typically worked in *pâte de verre*. This was easily broken, but its fragility was irrelevant since the pieces were designed to be ephemeral.

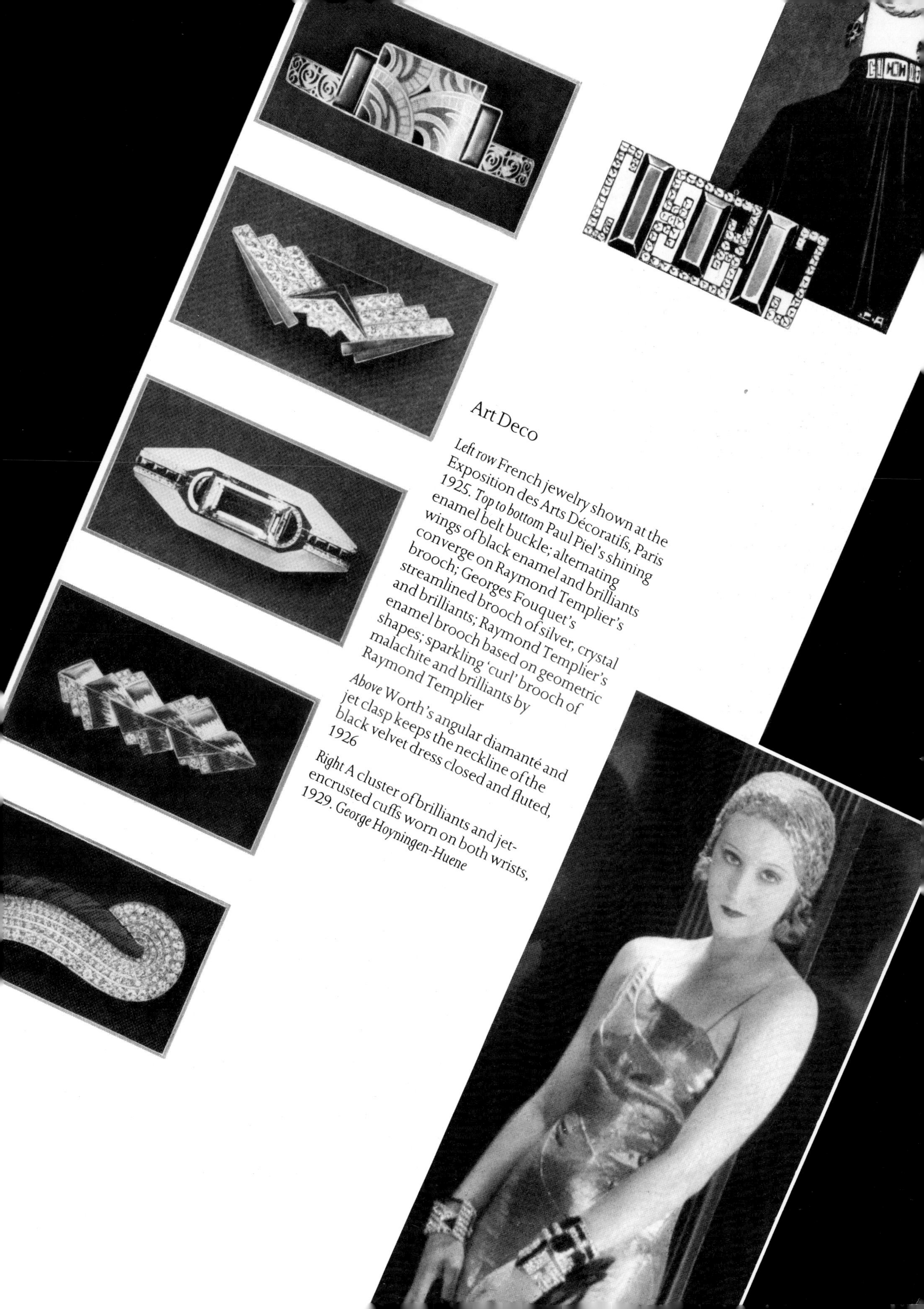

Art Deco

Left row French jewelry shown at the Exposition des Arts Décoratifs, Paris 1925. *Top to bottom* Paul Piel's shining enamel belt buckle; alternating wings of black enamel and brilliants converge on Raymond Templier's brooch; Georges Fouquet's streamlined brooch of silver, crystal and brilliants; Raymond Templier's enamel brooch based on geometric shapes; sparkling 'curl' brooch of malachite and brilliants by Raymond Templier

Above Worth's angular diamanté and jet clasp keeps the neckline of the black velvet dress closed and fluted, 1926

Right A cluster of brilliants and jet-encrusted cuffs worn on both wrists, 1929. *George Hoyningen-Huene*

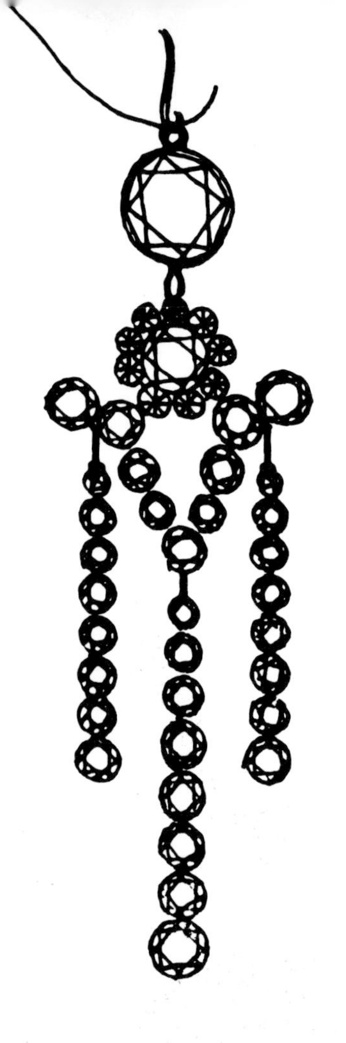

Long, pendulous earrings were all the rage in the mid-1920s. The ears and neck had become the centre of attention, thanks to the newly fashionable Eton crop and shingle, as well as the small-brimmed cloche hat and turban. All were part of the lean lines of the modern silhouette.

Left and right Selection of drop earrings from Palmyre's 1924 collection. *Left* Ornate pendant with coloured glass and stone imitating amethysts, rubies and emeralds; *right* elongated imitation pearl drop; diamanté and onyx tear-shaped drop, 1923

Below left Crystal drop earrings and necklace worn underneath a gold satin turban, 1924. *Wladimir Rehbinder*

Below centre A tortoise-shell crêpe dress, perfectly complemented by coral earrings and necklace, 1924. *Wladimir Rehbinder*

Below right Crystal drop earrings and necklace worn underneath a black velvet cloche, trimmed with ivory-coloured antique lace, 1924. *Havrah*

Opposite Molyneux's huge vine-leaf-shaped earrings of diamanté hung with tiny glass balls, 1923

Oak-leaf and acorn enamel necklace made by Gripoix for Chanel, 1938

Heavy, square Renaissance-style settings; pumpkin-shaped beads; glass flowers, like the miniature pansies later used to decorate Schiaparelli's scent bottles; and Maltese crosses, based on the Russian Grand Duke Dimitri's gift to Chanel, were the most typical of the Gripoix's work. An alternative to *pâte de verre* were Venetian patterned-glass beads imported from the long-established Murano glass-makers, Venini, and strung by Gripoix, who were masters of this new decorative art. Saks Fifth Avenue were so fascinated by their skills that they invited Mme Gripoix to sit in one of their windows making jewelry in full view of passers-by. But she refused to reveal the techniques by which she worked.

Fulco Santostefano della Cerda, duke of Verdura, the Sicilian painter, also worked with Chanel when he arrived in Paris in 1927. She employed him originally to design textiles, but he subsequently concentrated on costume jewelry. One of his first pieces for Chanel was a wide black and white enamel bracelet decorated with a multicoloured stone-encrusted Maltese cross, a piece which she often wore. In 1937 di Verdura emigrated to New York to design fine jewelry for Paul Flato and in 1939 opened his own fine jewelry business on Fifth Avenue.

Chanel's face brooch in gilt and coloured stone, c 1925. (*Billyboy Collection*)

Di Verdura's style inspired costume jewelry designers for three decades; Ken Lane and David Webb both credit his influence. He revived the interest in gold – women had consistently worn platinum and silver before the war – and enjoyed mixing real and semi-precious stones in Renaissance-style settings. He loathed the crude and ostentatious display of large solitaires and is reported to have criticized a fellow-guest at a party who was wearing a single, enormous sapphire, with the scathing aside, 'Minerology isn't jewelry.' Caning, knotting and bamboo details were other Verdura styles which were widely copied, for he set a trend in jewelry for many years. Society women, including the Duchess of Windsor and Elizabeth Payne Whitney, collected his novelties. Their appetite for his work was teasingly recalled in Cole Porter's Broadway song –

Liz Whitney has, on her
bin of manure, a
clip designed by the
Duke of Verdura.

Opposite Coco Chanel, photographed by Horst P. Horst in 1937, wearing a collection of gilt chains hung with large coins, cuffs of stone-encrusted gilt and matching earrings. All were to endure as fashion classics as was, of course, the little black dress

Like di Verdura, Chanel disapproved of ostentatious jewels but was ever scornful of meagre jewels. She would wear an entire bib, or vestee, of baubles round her throat and was singlehandedly responsible for the revival of pearls of all sizes, be they fake, cultured or natural. The development of cultured pearls and the perfection of imitation pearls, combined with Chanel's sanctioning of them, was the most distinctive costume jewelry

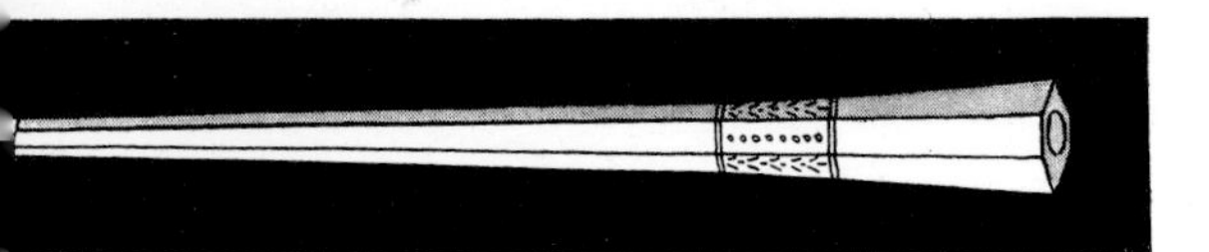

Above Cubist-style white cigarette holder traced with gold, by Audrey, 1927

Below Gloved hand, decorated with Art Deco bracelets, 1926

Opposite Costume jewels for Schiaparelli in 1937. *Left arm* Jean Schlumberger's flexible bracelet of jewelled cords, tied in a bow. On the wrist: Schiaparelli's imitation gold metal bracelet, like a close-fitting gauntlet, trimmed with a fringe of coloured stones. *Centre arm* Tchounsky's wide, layered bead bracelets, decorated with two elaborate mock-gold flowers; and Schiaparelli's baroque, gold-metal powder-puff. *Top* Delicate wild-rose clip of 'gold' bands with a faux-ruby centre above a Calla-lily clip, both by Schiaparelli. *Right arm* Schiaparelli's narrow chainmesh bracelet of mock-gold studded with coloured stones

trend of the twenties. Since the thirteenth century in China many attempts had been made to produce cultured pearls, but the first blister pearl was not successfully created until 1896, when Kokicho Mikimoto, a Japanese manufacturer, inserted an irritant into the oyster, around which the mollusc secreted its nacreous layers. The cultured, spherical pearl was perfected by 1915 and in 1921 introduced on to the London market, causing a dramatic fall in the price of natural pearls.

Fashionable society and the would-be fashionable middle classes welcomed this new invention for both its novelty and its relative cheapness. Many regarded the cultured pearl's surface as superior in sheen and smoothness to that of the natural pearl because the inserted bead was perfectly spherical and, if left for a sufficiently long time, could be covered in a very thick deposit. Furthermore, except by X-ray, it was impossible to tell the difference between a real and a cultured pearl.

The introduction of such apparently foolproof artificiality provoked tremendous snobbery. Loelia, Duchess of Westminster, considered that due caution and a sense of one's social position were essential in the wearing of cultured pearls; no woman should wear more artificial pearls than her husband could have afforded, were they real. Ostentatious deception she regarded as ill-placed and vulgar. However, Chanel's disregard for convention was an encouragement to many fashionable women to follow suit.

By 1927 French *Vogue* had acknowledged the importance of costume jewelry among the élite. There had been a period when the well-dressed woman would have been satisfied with a classic parure of pearls, diamonds and rare gems but 'today's stylish have decided to harmonise their jewelry with each one of their outfits.' But it was no longer a question of owning precious jewelry to suit each ensemble – a costly venture – but rather a variety of baubles. The demand for amber, jade and onyx, crystal, frosted crystal and brilliant crystal necklaces, *sautoirs*, bracelets, pins, belt buckles, handbag clasps, cigarette cases and earrings expanded dramatically. *Vogue* applauded the chicness of a young woman at a grand ball whose gown was simply embellished with crystal beads wrapped round her throat and wrists. 'This synthetic fashion, which is one of the typical symptoms of our time, is not without finesse, and that so many things are artificial – silk, pearls, furs – does not cease to make them chic.'

Plastic and synthetic jewelry were very fashionable in the twenties and thirties, satisfying the novelty-seeking element of the time. Numerous coloured and carved celluloid pieces were manufactured in imitation of the Art Deco jade and onyx jewelry from the fine jewelry houses. Bakelite had been tentatively introduced before the war but it was not until the twenties that it became highly fashionable, and the jeweler Auguste Bonas in particular

created a memorable collection of carved, faceted bracelets, bangles and necklaces in this material. In Milan Emma Caimi Pellini, who had established her business in 1928, designed Bakelite costume jewelry and glass and paste parures for various couture houses.

The United States market was the most receptive to novel costume jewelry, though American styles were, by and large, derivative of European themes, notably French, watered down for commercial acceptability. But some American designers did produce originals. Clothes designer Hattie Carnegie, for example, regularly accessorized her collections with eye-catching pieces. Miriam Haskell was one of the first to identify a market for well-made high-fashion costume jewelry. She envisaged that her client was accustomed to wearing real jewelry which, inevitably, unless she were extremely rich, would have to be worn again and again. From 1924 she sold from a salon in the exclusive McAlpine Hotel in New York. Her success was instant and Bernard Gimbel of Saks offered her a retail outlet in his store on Fifth Avenue. All the pieces, produced by her craftsman Frank Hess, were hand-made limited editions. They included baroque clusters of beads, floral themes and very elaborate clasps, as well as Chanel copies. Even during the lean Depression years, Haskell's business thrived.

American and Continental women welcomed the development of costume jewelry more readily than did their British counterparts, and they were able to purchase a wide range from department stores, US five-and-dime stores, street vendors and Continental 'parfumeries'. Trifari persuaded Alfred Philippe, who had worked for the fine jewelers Van Cleef & Arpels, to design for them and produced a range of tailored and novelty items for the mass market.

Modernism began to influence costume jewelry design by the late twenties. The emphasis, be it in sculpture, painting, jewelry, was on the medium – wood, steel, plastic – the process of production and technique and the 'honest' use of materials, underlining their intrinsic qualities. In jewelry it gave rise to sombre shapes and monochromatic colours, such as heavy, chain link bracelets in chrome, plastic and rhodium. Hard surfaces, rigid volumes and strident shapes became the new forms of costume jewelry, ousting coloured stones and filigree work. Louis Lozowick observed Modernism's infiltration into American design when he wrote in 1927, 'The dominant trend in America of today ... is towards order and organisation which find their outward sign and symbol in the rigid geometry of the American city: in the verticals of its smoke stacks, in the parallels of its car tracks, the squares of its streets, the cubes of its factories, the arc of its bridges, the cylinders of its gas tanks.' By the early thirties Modernist jewelry was widely worn.

Pair of black Bakelite and diamanté bangles; an onyx slave bangle; and dress rings, one inset with a pearl, the other with a tiny photograph frame. All from Rivoli, 1937

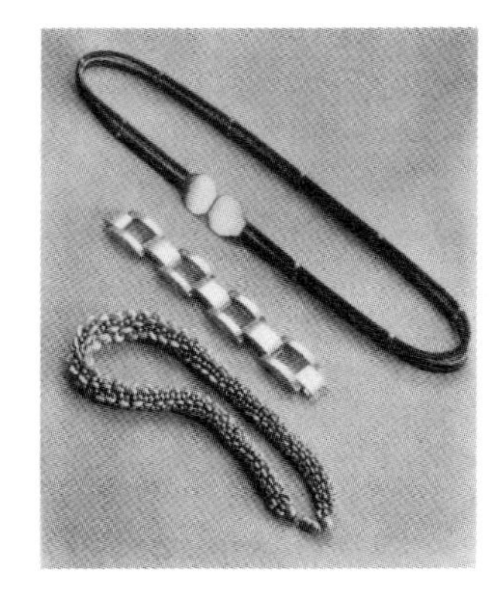

Above Gold metal spring belt from Saks Fifth Avenue; metal bracelet and a twisted necklace of gold beads, 1930. *Dana B. Merrill*

Opposite Schiaparelli's Surrealist jewelry (*from the Billyboy Collection*). Zodiac necklace with silver metal polychromatic symbols including two silver birds, two blue wolves, two purple men, two green men, two pink harps and yellow hair, by Jean Clément for Schiaparelli, 1938/9

While the postwar boom had encouraged modernity and originality in jewelry design, the subsequent Depression affected women's attitudes to costume jewelry in two contradictory ways. On the one hand, as fortunes crashed, women were no longer able to afford expensive jewelry. Many fine jewelers, finding themselves without employment, turned their talents to vigorous fakery with effective results. Consequently, costume jewelry benefitted not only from high standards of workmanship but also from greater artistic daring, to which the fashion-conscious were quick to respond.

Below and opposite The originality of Chanel's evening jewelry – as shown here in the imitation stone necklaces and bracelets from her 1927 collection – was the secret of its success. *Reading from top to bottom* Paste with black velvet; emerald glass and white satin; crackled red stones with banana velvet; paste with rose-coloured velvet; topaz with rose-beige satin, 1928

By contrast, arch conservatism and status-symbol, rather than novelty, dressing reassured a financially threatened society of its privileged position. Fashionable women turned to either modest 'estate' pieces or imitative 'good taste' jewelry, exemplified by strings of imitation pearls. Companies such as Ciro Pearls, established in 1917 in Britain to trade in real pearls, began to offer a wider and wider range of imitation single, double and triple strands, as well as restrained dress rings.

Multiple-function combination pieces which served many purposes were inevitably popular during such a thrifty era. Necklaces were designed which could be dismantled to form a pair of bracelets or brooches; brooches could be divided into a pair of dress clips. Interchangeable stones in rings provided a variety of colours to match different outfits.

Monocraft imitated gold so successfully that they too shifted their production to satisfy this conservative market. Founded in New York in 1930 by Michael Chernow, the company originally manufactured gilt initials for handbags, luggage and even cars, and did not turn to making costume jewelry until they were approached in 1936 by a department store buyer.

Despite Chanel's initiative and the consistent presentation of couture costume jewelry at most of the major European and American collections, costume jewelry continued to arouse suspicion within a certain coterie. In 1932 Princess Marthe Bibesco warned *Vogue* readers still suffering from the Depression that 'when it comes to wearing jersey, the uniform of the poor [a dig at Chanel], and the necklace of glass beads, a certain manner is indispensable, if [a duchess] is not to be mistaken for a shop girl.' Some sought financial security during the Depression and turned to fine 'investment' jewelry. By 1932 Chanel had done exactly this. According to Janet Flanner, the *New Yorker*'s Paris correspondent, 'With that aggravating instinct to strike when everyone else thinks the iron is cold, that has, up till now, made her a success, she has, at the height of the Depression, returned to precious stones as "having the greatest value in the smallest volume"; just as, during the boom, she launched glass gewgaws "because they are devoid of arrogance in an epoch of too easy luxe".'

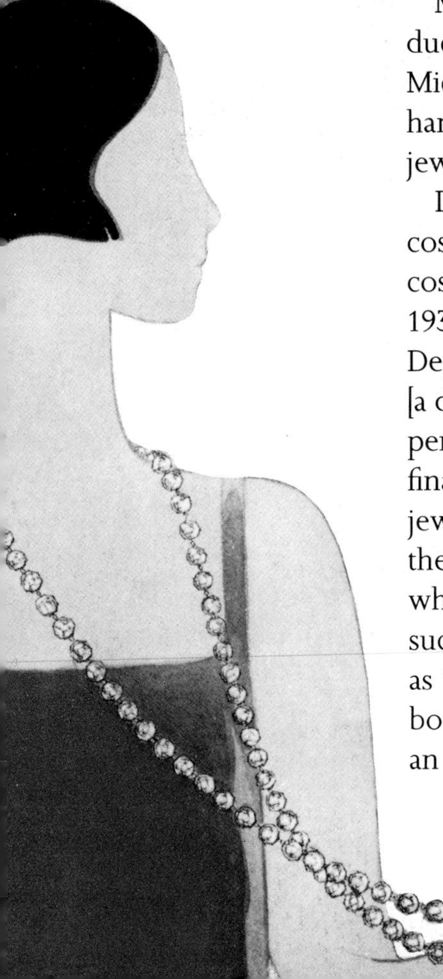

Modernism's 'clean-cut edge' brought with it a delight in the intrinsic qualities of materials – the grain of wood, the soapy patina of Bakelite, the faceted shine of gilt. Lewis Mumford saw the bold forms that emerged as a response to industrial machines with their 'hard surfaces, their rigid volumes, their stark shapes'. Such self-consciously Modernistic accessories were in tune with the militaristic clothes that marched through the international collections.

Opposite page, above left Cartier's dress watch, set in black enamel, 1935. *Horst P. Horst*

Far left Flexible gilt wristband with the added luxury of lapis lazuli, by Cartier, 1935. *Horst P. Horst*

Above right Jesse's grey, black and white enamel and crystal bracelet and belt buckle, 1934

Below Agate and amethyst set comprising brooch, ring, pair of dress clips and bracelet, by Herz, 1935. *Horst P. Horst*

This page Notched Bakelite ring suspended round the neck from a lace thong and worn with Alix's crêpe day dress, 1936. *Horst P. Horst*

Bright gilt, in bold, Modernistic forms – chains, tubes, links or discs – provided a focal point to the ubiquitous black city dress. This jewelry was usually confined to the neck and wrists; eye-catching earrings were *de trop*, as the contemporary mode concentrated on dramatic millinery.

Left Lelong's gilt snake chains wound loosely round the neck of his plain black dress, 1938

Below A linked gilt necklace of interlocking circles complements Piguet's woollen dress and Boy's triangular folded black taffeta hat, 1936

Opposite Highly polished gilt coin bracelet, 1944. *Norman Parkinson*

Above Schiaparelli's 'Egg' necklace of oval white beads, 1931, and Adrian Mann's blond bead necklace, 1971. *Barry Lategan*

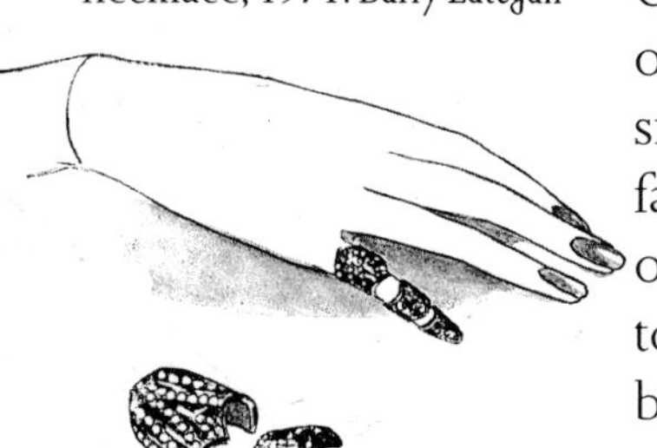

Above Count Etienne de Beaumont's set of three finger rings, one covering the nail, for Schiaparelli, 1938. *E. Lindner*

Opposite, above right Gilded metal brooch inspired by a Dali painting, *c* 1938. *Near left* Gold plastic composite mermaid brooch attributed to Dali, *c* 1937. *Below left* Gold-plated metal mussel shell brooch decorated with 'gold' metal balls, attributed to Jean Schlumberger for Schiaparelli, *c* 1937-9. *Below right* Jean Schlumberger's unicorn brooch for Schiaparelli, in silver metal, diamanté and black paint, signed Schiaparelli, *c* 1937. (*All from the Billyboy Collection*)

Elsa Schiaparelli was also to tease and shock the fashionable public. Embracing the contemporary art movements – Dadaism and Surrealism – she gave contemporary expression to her collections while perfectly 'matchmaking' the clothes and the costume jewelry. Surrealist touches on her strict, tailored, black suits included peanut-, padlock- or musical-note-shaped buttons, and hatchet-and-heart-shaped brooches. Schiaparelli even offered a gadget to be worn on the lapel which lit up at night and diamond-studded false fingernails. She explained to *Vogue* that 'Working with artists like Christian Bérard, Jean Cocteau, Salvador Dali, Marcel Vertès and Kees van Dongen . . . one felt supported and understood beyond the crude and boring reality of merely making a dress sell.'

The earliest examples of Schiaparelli costume jewelry were seen in 1931: feather, ermine and porcelain flower necklaces made by Count Etienne de Beaumont, who had switched allegiance from Schiaparelli's major rival, Chanel. In 1931 *Vogue* admired her 'egg' necklace, made from white beads on a black thong. By the following year Jean Clément had been commissioned to design unusual metal clips that slipped through button holes to fasten her tailored suits, while in 1935 Schiaparelli mocked the devaluation of the franc by producing a series of gold sovereign and French louis buttons. Celebrating the Christmas festivities of 1937, she fastened a range of blouses with Christmas tree and chocolate titbit buttons by Salvador Dali.

In 1933 *Vogue* photographed Schiaparelli wearing Surrealist, snail-shaped jewels by Herz; a simple black dress such as she wore on this occasion was the most usual canvas for her Surrealist fantasies. From her artist friends she soon commissioned some memorable pieces which have become widely copied classics: in 1937 Salvador Dali created telephone ear 'rings' and Jean Cocteau a lacquered, eye-shaped brooch, with a suspended pearl tear; Jean Schlumberger produced a dagger-pierced-heart brooch after those that were popular in Europe in the fourteenth and fifteenth centuries, and the poet Louis Aragon a necklace hung with aspirin. Jean Clément's passion thermometers indicated to a lover one's excitement, 'from frustration point upwards'. Both Schlumberger's sunbeam brooch with gilt rays studded with diamanté and Dali's plastic-winged bee became classic pieces.

Schiaparelli utilized a wide and varied range of materials: feathers, paperweights, chains, locks,clips, lollipops, ceramic bracelets on raffia cords, huge industrial chains, fake glass (Rhodophane) and rubber. Novelty buttons – some of wood and others of plastic – were a distinguishing house feature and were copied by other couturiers, but without the original flourish. 'Along with these our own unusual jewelry of enamelled ivory necklaces went like lightning,' recalled Schiaparelli, 'as did the first plexiglass bracelet and earrings. They were designed by men of extraordinary talent,

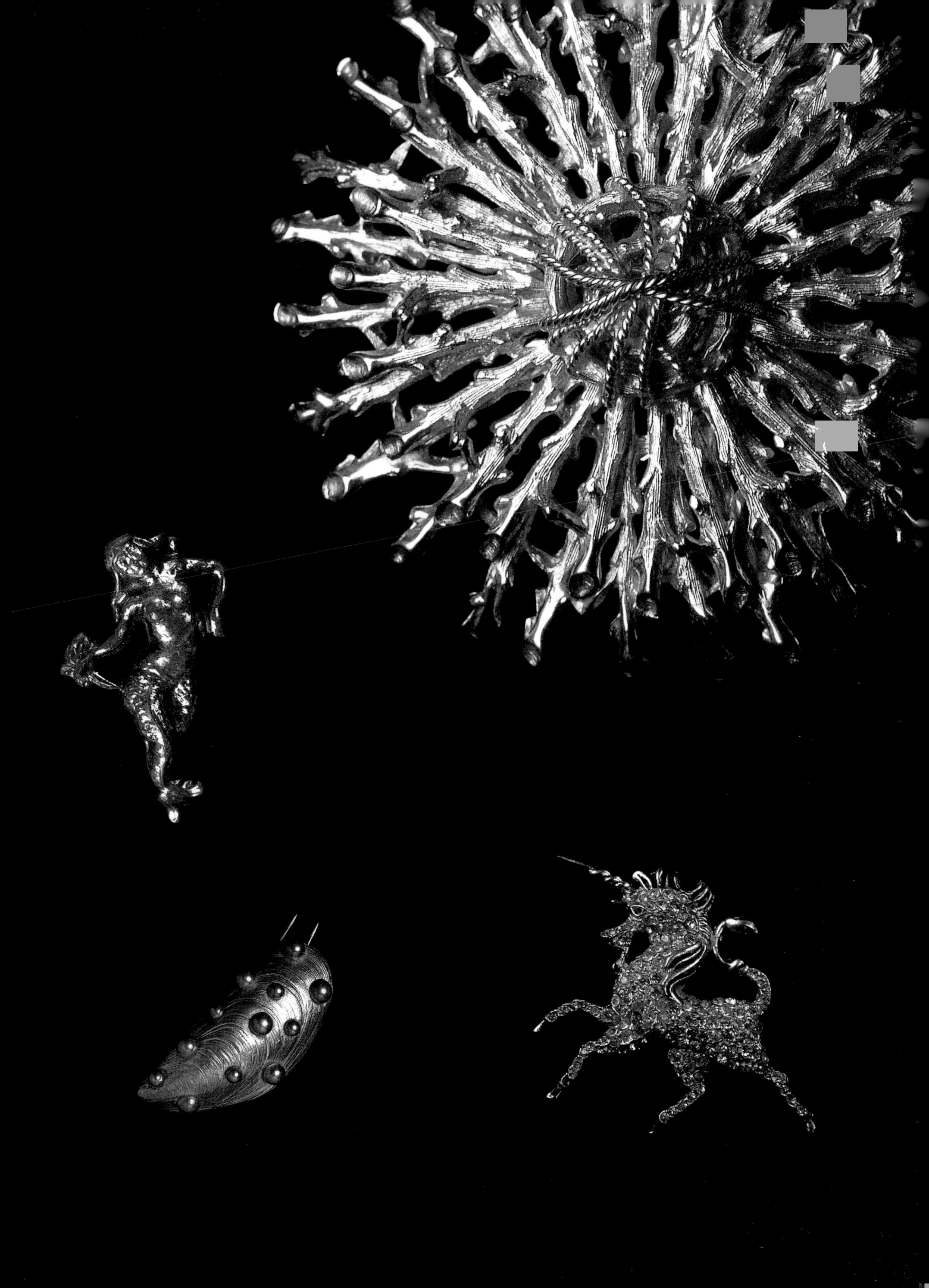

La Gaieté du
CIRQUE
a inspiré
SCHIAPARELLI:
les motifs,
les formes,
les couleurs,
les paillettes.

such as Jean Clément, a genius in his way, a real French artisan, who would work with such burning love that he was almost a fanatic.' Her net of collaborators spread wide, from the society photographer Cecil Beaton and the artist Jean Hugo (grand-nephew of Victor Hugo) to Christian Bérard who designed plastic fish bracelets.

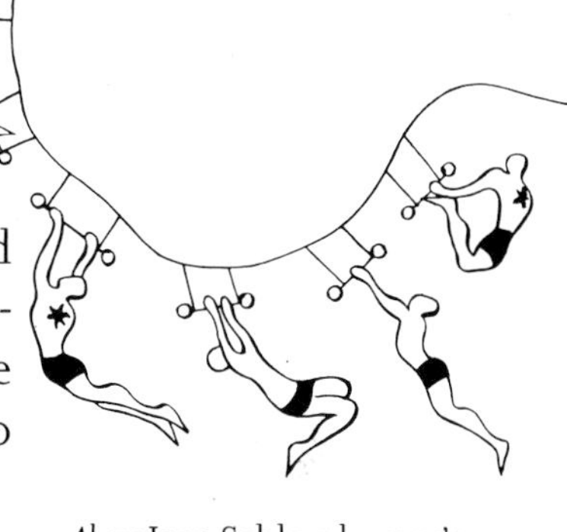

Above Jean Schlumberger's painted tin circus necklace, 1938

Despite her consistent patronage of fellow-artists, Schiaparelli's collaboration was often selfish. Jean Schlumberger attracted her attention with his diamond-studded and gold-encased porcelain flowers, of the kind that decorate eighteenth-century chandeliers or Sèvres porcelain. She summoned him to her office and he began to create pieces from junk markets and old Victorian castings. However, despite the attention that he gained the house, with such memorable work as his heart chains, rollerskate brooches and snake hatpins, Schiaparelli refused to acknowledge to the press his (or any other designer's) rôle in accessorizing her clothes. She insisted that the house's output be united under one name, 'Schiaparelli', and when *Vogue* credited Schlumberger in the magazine, both he and the editor were severely chastised for disloyalty.

Above Dali's influence in costume jewelry prevailed throughout the century, as shown in these old-gold-coloured sunburst earrings by Gary Wright and Sheila Teigue, 1984. *Paul Lange*

Below Schiaparelli's red enamel heart clip stabbed with 4 gilt swords, 1939

Nineteen-thirty-six was *the* Surrealist fashion year. Anything could stimulate an idea for costume jewelry in Schiaparelli's mind. She once produced a stone brooch which reflected the formation of moles on her cheek. She would often design one-off pieces for herself, such as a knitted woollen band tied round the neck from which hung a row of tin can-can dancers' legs. Theme puns would make up a collection: the 'Circus Collection' of Spring 1938, for example, which consisted of Christian Bérard's circus printed fabrics tailored into jackets and skirts accessorized by little tin brooches and pins depicting can-can legs and clowns' heads; or the Harlequin collection of Autumn 1938, which featured painted plaster masks by Jean Clément. Gold hearts on leather wrist straps; brooches depicting gingerbread pigs, baby elephants, fruits, fish and horsedrawn Roman chariots; nappy/diaper pins and curtain ring scarf clips (1932); Clément's brilliants-encrusted ostriches, sportswear cameos, lantern brooches that actually lit up and face jewelry, such as glassless spectacles – all these amused Schiaparelli and were snapped up by her novelty-hungry audience, which included such capricious society leaders as Mrs Reginald Fellows, Mae West and Lady Elsie Mendl.

Opposite In Schiaparelli's Circus Collection the silhouettes, textile prints and details – right down to the buttons and jewelry – were inspired by the circus. Schiaparelli sewed prancing horse-, juggler- and clown-face buttons to her couture collection of 1938

Mae West was one of many Hollywood stars whose bejewelling in the popular films of the thirties and forties also lent credence to the use of costume jewelry. Art Deco motifs associated with Hollywood, such as palm trees, sunbursts and fountains, were worn and the glamourous combination of white gold and diamonds, favoured by film stars, found its way into costume jewelry.

Dress clips, invariably worn in pairs, were considered the most fashionable jewelry of the 1930s. They could draw attention to the bodice, highlight the edge of a neckline, fasten a gathering of material or simply decorate a cloth belt.

Opposite, centre Dark, silk jumper decorated with diamanté clips at each side of the neck, echoing the tiny clip on the velvet headband, 1939. *John Rawlings*

Above Trifari's top-hat-stick-and-gloves clip in black enamel and rhinestones, 1938

Below Trifari's anemone clip of enamel with rhinestone-tipped petals, 1938

Far right Gaston's black woollen coatdress of printed crêpe cinched at the waist with a half-moon mother-of-pearl clasp, 1938

Above Asprey's dazzling 'clipmate' brooch of rhinestones with burning faux-ruby centres, 1936. *George Miles*

Centre Henri Kahn's double clips in brilliants, 1937. *Chevoson*

Below A gleaming enamel mosaic clip holds the jabot of Hartnell's black-and-silver striped lamé afternoon dress, 1934. *Horst P. Horst*

Chanel's ethnic-style gilt bib necklace and matching earrings, 1939. *Roger Schall*

Charm bracelets hung with decorative seals, many based on old English coats of arms, became particularly fashionable in the mid-thirties. Schiaparelli had introduced them because they reminded her of her grandfather's watch chain. Engraved crystal and stone-ornamented gilt seals and intaglios clanked on many a fashionable wrist. Similarly, both Schiaparelli and Chanel favoured gilt coin necklaces and bracelets. By 1937 Chanel was advocating entire vestees of glittering coins hanging down the bodice of a plain black dress. To accompany the tailored suits of the mid-thirties, *Vogue* approved the substantial gilt chain bracelet or gauntlet-like cuff fringed with coloured stones, worn over the glove. Cartier, Herz and many of the French fashion houses offered these trinkets.

By the late thirties, the American market was the most varied and competitively priced; Trifari, Cohn & Rosenberger, Boucher, Pennino and Haskell being market leaders. Irene Parkes, chief buyer of costume jewelry at Harrods, made an annual voyage to New York on the *Queen Mary* to buy a year's supply of jewelry. During those years of international autarky, she was limited by an import quota to buying only a small range – 'a matter of hundreds rather than thousands of pounds worth'. As an enthusiastic new recruit at Harrods she had observed that Ciro pearls had applied for the entire national import quota on costume jewelry; there were no other takers. She challenged this, ensuring a fair share for Harrods.

Double-clip brooches and bracelets were Harrods best sellers. Once a line became fashionable at Cartier, for example, it would filter right down the market and achieve mass popularity; Trifari would copy Cartier and, in turn, would be copied by Corocraft and eventually by Woolworth. Trifari's three most popular pieces throughout the thirties were the crown brooch, a collectable Trifari classic, which came in two sizes, brooches and dress clips set with hexagonally shaped stones and oblong, modernistic link bracelets and necklaces.

Indian ethnic jewelry was revived in the mid-thirties, notably in the United States. Leading department stores stocked gilt filigree pendulous earrings and collars, some set with tiny stones. Mexican jewelry, made by the talented Rebajes, was also a fashionable alternative. Pieces by Rebajes have become very collectable, especially in America.

By 1937 curves and flowers supplemented the hard lines of Art Deco and Modernism. Flower spray and bouquet jewelry, with a gilded finish, were studded with coloured glass stones, imitating petals, while Schiaparelli popularized enamel flower pins.

The Second World War affected the costume and fine jewelry trade in much the same way as the First World War. Many costume jewelry factories, offering metalwork and precision instrument facilities, were converted for

Kitsch

Above Digby Morton's set of crystal star hair clips, 1934. *George Miles*

Right Miss Foster's turquoise lizard clip, 1941

Below Mock-porcelain multipurpose bracelet, to hold money, makeup and aspirins, 1939. *John Rawlings*

Above right D. Nossiter's mesh of faux-rubies, -emeralds and -pearls encircling the entire ear, 1940. *George Miles*

Below right Paquin's Victorian-style posy brooch – flowers on a broderie anglaise frill with a sprinkling of leather hearts, 1941. *Lee Miller*

The War Look

Left A semi-circlet of crystal squares is attached to the neckline of Franklin Simon's black halter-neck dress, to match the earrings, 1945. *Irving Penn*

Above A fob hanging from a gold lamé belt dresses up a simple black dinner gown, 1945. *Frances McLaughlin*

war requirements. Metal castings, bullets, surgical steel equipment and radio components were manufactured in converted factories. Although gold and silver bullion were in short supply, affecting fine jewelry production, costume jewelry was not rationed on either side of the Atlantic. It was, nevertheless, not as widely available because both manpower and materials, such as base metals, were in short supply. Many companies were forced to use sterling silver as a substitute for white metals now conscripted by the government. Others, like Miriam Haskell, used wood, leather or beads as alternatives.

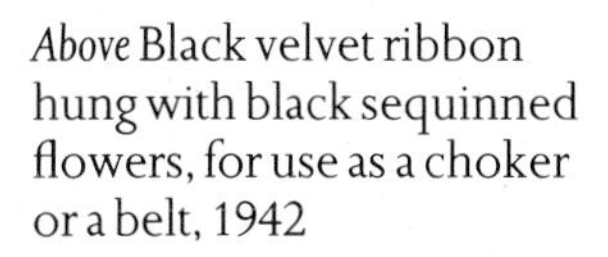

Above Black velvet ribbon hung with black sequinned flowers, for use as a choker or a belt, 1942

Below Mme Manzi Fé's black lace snood sequinned with butterflies, 1944

Many of the jewelry factories in Europe were centred in main industrial towns, such as Birmingham in Britain and Pforzheim in Germany, with the result that during the war several were badly bombed. During the German occupation Czechoslovakian stones became very scarce and few were exported. Consequently, jewelers had to rely on rations or the black market. Fried Frères, based in Paris, were forced to make their own jewelry rather than depend on supplies.

Irene Parkes of Harrods recalls that it was extremely difficult to get costume jewelry for her department during the war; very little was being made in Britain and absolutely none was imported. As an alternative she started to search out and stock antique pieces such as pinchback, Whitby jet, Berlin iron jewelry and Victoriana, which she found for reasonable prices in markets across the country. Dreary regimental badges, which catered for an understandable need, were manufactured in Birmingham. Plastic jewelry was also available but because of its crude mass production could hardly imbue an outfit with the glamour of a diamanté or gilt piece.

After the war, Trifari decided to guide the market away from its acquired taste for sterling silver, which tarnished and was too expensive. The company came up with an alternative, 'Trifarium', which was marketed as a secret formula. The marketing process was successful enough to convert the fashion-conscious public to white metals.

The era between the wars had proved to be rich in both imagery and the use of unexpected materials. By contrast, costume jewelry of the immediate postwar years was to flaunt the opulence and glamour of eighteenth-century style and look to allure rather than novelty.

Right Veiled black felt pillbox with aviator badge (from Black, Starr & Gorham), by Altman's, 1942. *John Rawlings*

3 · 1946 – 1964

Universal Acceptance: Baroque Paste, Gilt and Plastic by Day and Night

Imitation, rather than innovation, characterized costume jewelry for almost a decade after the war. The revival of eighteenth-century-style paste and instant copies of fine gems nourished a market hungry for expensive-looking glitz. If Bulgari came out with a solid gold link bracelet, or Cartier with a jewelled and enamelled blackamoor, within a few weeks the costume jewelry version followed. The Americans were especially proficient at the rapid manufacture of copies. There was, in fact, a two-way exchange between fine and costume jewelers, as designers moved from one field to the other, bringing ideas and skills with them.

Diana Vreeland was personally responsible for one collaboration, described in her memoirs.

'Have I ever shown you my little blackamoor heads from Cartier with their enamelled turbans? Baba Lucinge and I used to wear them in rows and rows . . . they were the chic of Paris in the late thirties. When I moved to New York I made arrangements for Paris Cartier to sell them to New York Cartier, and all I can tell you is that the *race* across the ocean – this was by boat, don't forget – was something fierce. The Cartier ones were quite expensive, but then Saks brought out a copy of them that sold for something like, in those days, thirty dollars a piece and it was impossible to tell them apart. So I bought the copies and wore them with the real ones, like decorations – I was *covered* in blackamoors.'

In the forties, the war-torn West trusted in gold and precious stones; their value as an immutable, international currency had been sustained despite hostilities. Perhaps it was a craving for stability that led to the popularity of heavy, ostentatious gold jewelry. This taste filtered down into the imitation jewelry market and craftsmen and factories in Europe and America specialized in imitation-gold pieces, the best of which were gilded in three different shades to give a textured effect. Trifari prided themselves on this technique, claiming to have the finest gilders in the business.

Above René Boivin's gilded and bejewelled blackamoor carrying a bowl of fruit, 1949. *Arik Nepo*

Opposite Lavender, purple and pink strands of beads by Gripoix for Dior, 1954. *Horst P. Horst*

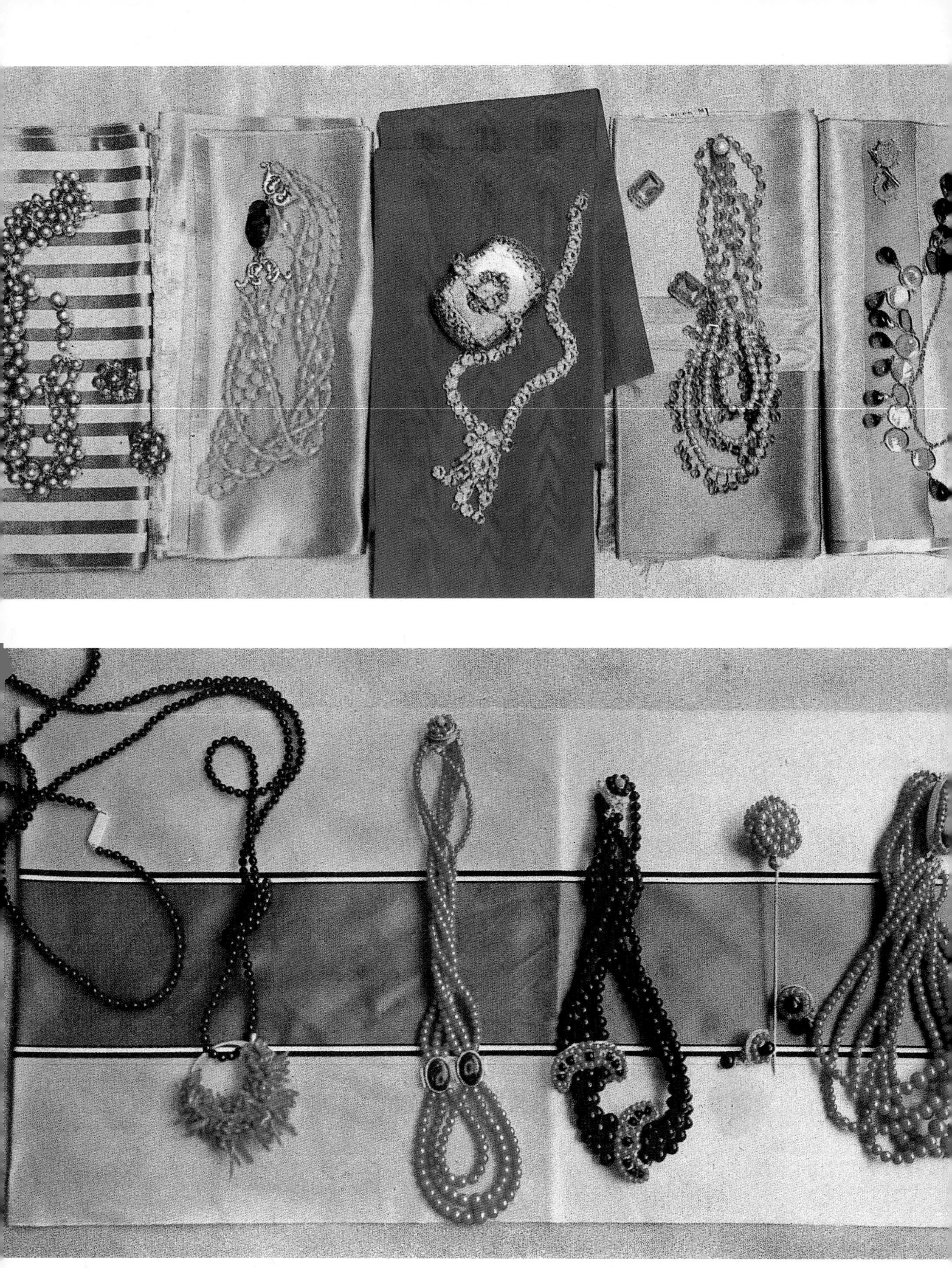

Fashion designers and customers alike craved luxury and formality. After years of blackouts and austerity, women donned glittering jewelry to add sparkle to the social scene. As evening wear in particular became richer, more formal and colourful, so did the accompanying jewels. From Fifth Avenue to the avenue Montaigne, gems or paste not only accessorized grand evening toilettes but actually became part of them; stones were set into the embroidered waistband of a dinner gown, or were used to ornament the sleeves of an opera coat, the shoulders of an evening wrap or the hem of a ball gown.

Norman Hartnell, the London couturier noted for his designs for members of the royal family, welcomed the return to ritual, formality and splendour, at which the British, he believed, were masters. In 1946 he wrote in *Argentor*, the journal of the National Jewellers Association, that the very fabrics themselves were dyed in jewel-like colours – ruby-red and emerald-green – and jewel motifs, such as a scattering of stones or gold chain swags, were printed on to the cloth.

The shapes and details of both fine and costume jewelry were conventional and traceably retrospective, echoing the mood in contemporary clothes design. Just as women wore Edwardian-style cinched corsets, Victorian-inspired bell skirts, muffs and button boots, so were they decorated with Renaissance, Empire (from 1948), Victorian and Edwardian jewelry motifs and shapes.

One break with tradition, evident among all this formality, was that of wearing sparkling jewelry by day as well as by night; it was no longer vulgar to pin a diamond or diamanté brooch to an outfit before the cocktail hour, for now even tailored suits sported glitter – a trick that Schiaparelli had introduced in the thirties but which few had seriously adopted then. Couturiers consequently designed clothes which displayed fine or costume jewelry with panache: racing suits were cut with breast pockets to feature a pocket brooch – the earthy, autumnal colours of the tweed reflected in the gold chains and chokers set with Cairngorm, topaz or tourmaline stones; day frocks featured 'bracelet-length' sleeves, designed to reveal the forearm fashionably laden with jangling bracelets, while plunging *décolletés* were scissored into evening dresses to frame an important parure, or were cut away from the shoulders to feature a pair of dress clips. Many houses presented jewelled buttons; Charles Creed's tweed suits, for example, were buttoned with gold seals, linked, one to the other, by gilt fob chains.

Not only was the little black dress brought to life with eye-catching trinkets, but costume jewelry had its own 'little black dresses' – the essential versatile pieces – such as a rope of pearls or a single delicate cluster of fruit or flowers worn as importantly as a precious stone.

Dior's mammoth brilliants necklace, worn with a red wool day dress, 1947. *Erwin Blumenfeld*

Opposite, top row, from left to right Paquin's aquamarine and grey beads; Dessès's amber-tinted crystal twist; Piguet's topaz choker; Dessès's three rows of pearl and topaz with matching earrings; Fath's two-toned topaz chain. *Bottom row* Selection from Coppola and Toppo, for Schiaparelli: jet and coral in twisted bead necklaces with heavy clasps; matching earrings and hatpin, 1949. *Richard Rutledge*

Left Piguet's black crêpe dress worn with a long string of pearls, under Reboux's dramatic, asymmetrical black velvet hat, 1950

Right Balmain's white curly lambswool scarf embroidered with imitation pearls, 1947. *Don Honeyman*

During the forties *Vogue* reported on the variety of couture novelties used at each collection to enhance the silhouette. A rhinestone pin at the gathering point of swagged drapery, a bar brooch along a prominent seam or a paste pin at the base of a deep *décolleté*, could draw attention to the distinguishing features of a gown. A scooped evening neckline could be spotlit with Schiaparelli's off-the-shoulder rhinestone necklace or Piguet's pearl choker with an additional strand, which traced the edge of the neckline, caught by a chatelaine. Balmain's feminine novelties included curly lambswool scarves embroidered with pearls, bracelets made by pinning a folded handkerchief with a brooch to the wrist, and pearls which pushed up the winged collar of a blouse.

Dior revived unmitigated femininity and conspicuous luxury. Ripping out shoulder pads, raising heel heights, lowering necklines and adding touches of blatant allure, such as precariously tilted picture hats, white gloves and ornamental umbrellas, he challenged the notions of physical freedom and practicality in dress advanced during the war. A woman was supposed to proclaim her sex and act as a decorative adjunct to her escort. Jewelry was an important aspect of this look. Rich, albeit fake, jewelry underlined woman's sparkling, though inconsequential, rôle.

Accompanying the success of Dior's 'New Look' in 1947 came iridescent paste, echoing the taste of the French eighteenth-century court. Much of it was designed by Mme Gripoix, who recalls working through the night to complete the large collection of 'New Look' jewels. Ornate diamanté chandelier earrings matched equally dazzling necklaces; for day, cut-glass pin 'explosions' decorated pert tailored suits.

The Little Black Dress

Above Griffe's swathe of chiffon folded into an enormous bow and highlighted by a glistening band of diamanté, 1955. *Guy Bourdin*

Left A long, ornate diamanté fob gathers in the black satin of Dior's evening dress, 1955. *Henry Clarke*

Just as Dior's 'Envol' (winged) and 'Zig Zag' collections of 1948 delighted in asymmetrical flightiness – created by flying panels, side-scooped skirts and jutting collars or cuffs – so did the accompanying jewelry affect off-centredness and movement. Necklaces hung at a slant across the poitrine, dripping with stones suspended at one side; a single long earring would be worn or a pair of tailored clips on one ear, while stone-decorated flower or animals were attached to springs, creating a 'tremblant' effect.

By 1948, Byzantine colour had become an important factor. *Vogue* praised the rainbow hues of Dior's Indian bangles (worn several at a time), stone chip necklaces and sequins. Piguet showed a raw yellow necklace hung with garnet-red drops, Dior a fiery, ruby-red oval choker interspersed with rhinestones.

The alliance between fashion and jewelry continued, and editorials encouraged women and designers alike to refer to the precedent set by the Elizabethans, who had achieved a perfect integration of jewels, fabric and embroidery in every grand toilette. However, caution was urged, to avoid a clash between an elaborately sequinned and embroidered dress and over-ornate jewelry.

A fashionably dressed woman was expected to own a range of jewelry, both real and fake: large single-stone rings, chunky dress clips, massive bracelets, dangling earrings and large earclips. Hair ornaments, too, became essential, as the dressed coiffure returned to high fashion. A woman would have been considered ungroomed, at any time of the day, without at least some of these. Pablo of Elizabeth Arden even designed a tracery of glittering paillettes to adorn sandal straps and decorative flowers to wear between the toes.

In general, clip earrings were worn by day and dangling earrings by night and both would have been clip or screw fitted, as pierced ears were considered barbaric. Chandelier, diamanté necklaces highlighted deep *décolletés*; indeed, those from the shop Paris House were made from the crystal drops of an original Georgian chandelier. The sophisticated gamine haircut, fashionable from 1948, called for long and elaborate earrings to trace the line of the bared neck. The hairstyle was in fact created by Coppola Toppo to show off just such heavy pieces of jewelry. Even fine jewelry houses offered fashion jewelry novelties; Asprey's brooch made of a washable bunch of plastic grapes was a great success in 1949.

Opposite page, left Givenchy's baroque pearl and diamanté brooch is pinned to the plunging silk moiré collar of his jersey evening gown. A matching bracelet is worn, 1954. *Sante Forlano*

Above Schiaparelli's tinted, square-cut rhinestones stand away from the neck to decorate the expansive *décolleté*, 1958. *Clifford Coffin*

Centre Piguet's pearl choker, a free-falling strand caught by a chatelaine, traces the neckline, 1948. *Clifford Coffin*

Below Lanvin-Castillo's 'bijoux-cravat' of satin, diamanté and pearl, 1955. *Guy Bourdin*

Right Fath's navy-blue shantung, accordion-pleated, button-through dress with two enormous rhinestone pins fastened to one revers, 1951. *John Rawlings*

The hair ornament – a lighter touch than the cocktail hat – was worn in the evening, drawing the hair off the forehead to focus attention on dramatic doe-eyed makeup and painted lips. Diamanté, velvet and satin Alice bands were balanced on neat chignons, French pleats or short coiffures, to create a demure yet *soigné* air.

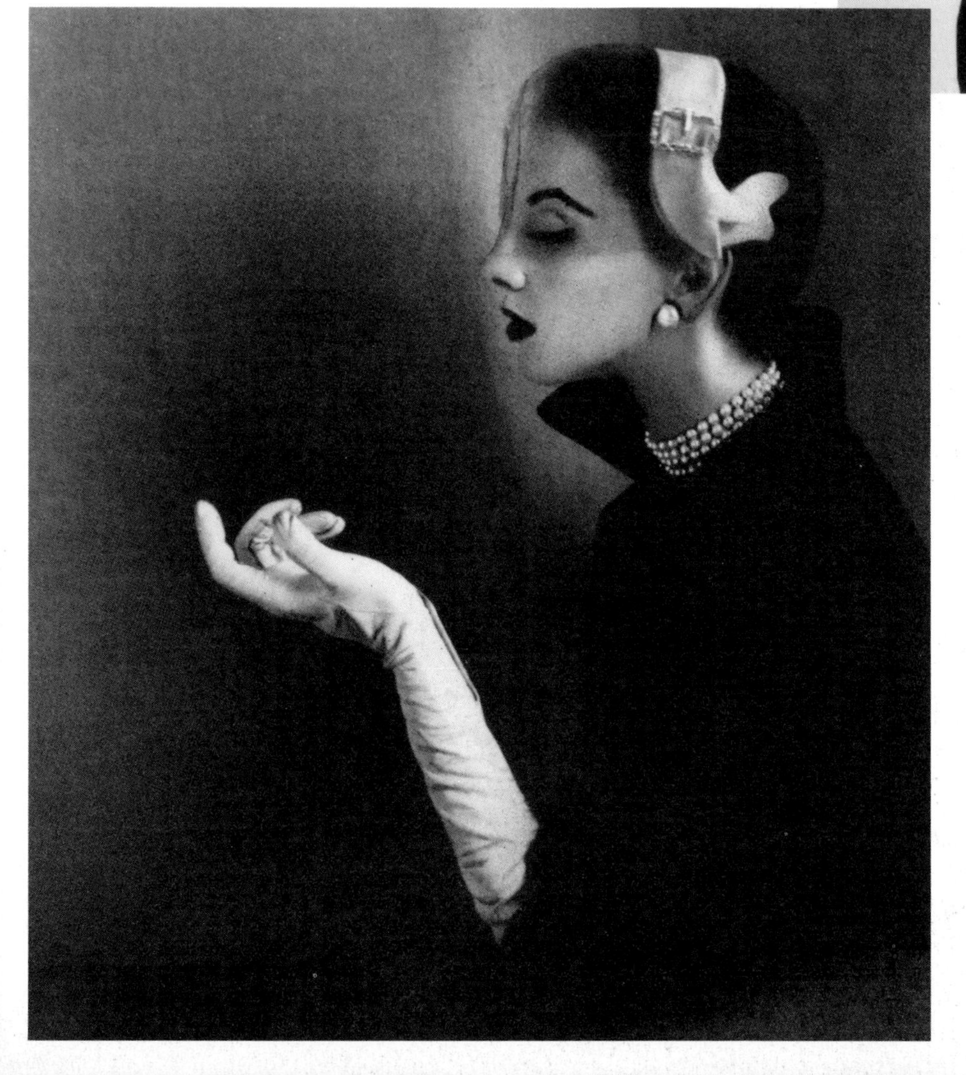

Above Grecian hairstyle and ornament by Paulette – a lightweight tangle of gilt; grass and leaves coil round the head, tracing the hairline, 1955. *Henry Clarke*

Left Worn tightly on a close-cropped head – Svend's pale apricot satin 'belt' ribbon with rhinestone buckle, 1955. *Guy Bourdin*

Opposite Rébés's pearl and sequin hair ornament, with tiny feathers which curl over the head, framing the face, 1955. *Guy Bourdin*

Left De Roben's chain hung with silver coins to be worn as a necklace or threaded through a belt, 1946. *Frances McLaughlin*

Distinct national traits in the use of costume jewelry were maintained; the French and the Americans embraced its revival but the British maintained a dignified, conservative resistance to this 'cheap' mode. Charles Creed, a leading British couturier, informed *Argentor* readers in 1948 that costume jewelry was, quite correctly, still frowned upon among the well-dressed in Britain. It was 'a heartening sign', he claimed, 'that the quantity of junk jewelry – so popular before the war – has considerably diminished in recent years.' Parisians, on the other hand, loved faux gems and almost every couturier gave his blessing to bold, though essentially classical, costume jewelry. On both sides of the Atlantic gilt chain bracelets and necklaces, many hung with seals or coins – of the kind that accompanied the black tailored suits of the 1930s – were worn with casual coordinates.

Vogue suggested that costume jewelry could enliven an old wardrobe as well as being the starting point of a new one. 'It could be a new use of jewelry – a theatrically big brooch on the hip (Dior), a small pair pinned to the cuffs of a suit, or even jewelled buttons worn as cufflinks (Fath). A string of pearls can be wound round a chignon, or a rhinestone buckle fasten a belt.' Editorials encouraged readers to search out pretty buttons to adorn sports blouses or use slave bangles or encase a throat in glass beads.

Vogue teased and surprised its audience by using costume jewelry in unconventional ways. Hugh Allen, the Sales Director of Trifari in the United States, recalls how *Vogue* editors rarely chose to feature the commercial lines, such as conservative dress pins or tailored gilt earrings, preferring the most avant-garde pieces. And they would alter the use of a piece in a cavalier manner, linking three diamanté bracelets to form a necklace or spraying a seed pearl bracelet gold, thereby confusing the reader, who could never find 'the necklace' or 'the bracelet I saw in *Vogue*' in the stores. But it was *Vogue*'s role to show that costume jewelry should not be taken too seriously. It was there to be played with and enjoyed.

Most couture boutiques, by contrast, displayed the evocative yet ephemeral frivolities of each season's look with the care accorded to royal gems. Dior's boutique in Paris, which was 'papered, plastered, boothed and hung with brown-inked toile de Jouy, a scene of elegant rusticity', offered jewels and beads displayed on satin-lined, straw bread baskets or on dressed cane dummies. The most exclusive couture pieces were set in sterling silver rather than a tin alloy. By the end of the fifties most of the Dior costume jewelry was designed by his young *protégé*, Yves Saint Laurent.

Opposite Cut-glass stone, imitation pearl and gilt jewelry by Henry à la Pensée, Gripoix and Francis Winter, 1957. *William Klein*

OVERLEAF

Left page On the left, Dior's pale blue linen jacket, embroidered with bird motifs and encrusted with pearls and rhinestones, worn over a black sheath dress. On the right, Lafaurire's metal-grey linen dress and cape, patterned with clusters of blue sequins, 1948. *Des Russell*

Right page Frank Usher's exotic evening coat in Moygashel print embroidered with raffia thread, glittering topaz and rhinestone beads, 1964. *David Bailey*

Off the grand boulevards, numerous French craftsmen were to be found who supplied the Paris fashion houses with magnificent jewelry. In her 1956 book *Paris à la Mode*, Celia Bertin recalls visiting some of these. One of the leading craftsmen was Francis Winter, the President of the Chambre Syndicale des Paruriers. He produced 2,500 models a year which were divided, as were the clothes they accessorized, into four collections. These were first shown in Paris to his regular couture customers (many of whom demanded exclusive rights) and then sold to department stores or smaller houses at home and abroad.

'The weighty décor is pure Balzac,' writes Celia Bertin of Winter's atelier, 'or, anyway, typically French – sombre, good, unostentatious. Here in France, prosperity is unobtrusive. I went to one of the showcases, and there amongst a parure of artificial diamonds, a *rivière* necklace, a baguette bracelet, and a long chain set with imitation emeralds, I recognised things I had seen in the boutique of one of the couturiers.'

Earring created for Dior by Francis Winter in strass and coloured stones with an adjustable fitting, 1953. *Robert Randall*

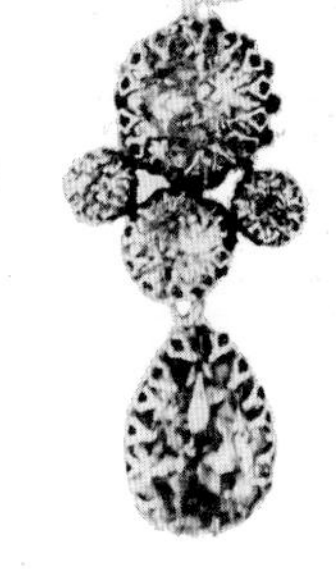

Leaving the atelier, Miss Bertin concluded that 'extremely ornate jewelry that recalls a bygone age is once again in fashion and there is plenty of work in the ateliers: but I am surprised to see these luxurious, mock-precious trifles being made in the overpoweringly heavy surroundings proper to a Carné film. It is all so odd, so gloomy.'

Winter's thriving business employed sixty craftsmen, each specializing in woodwork, metalwork or stone cutting. With the usual exception of gilding, all the work was completed in the workshop. These craftsmen did not work in isolation but consulted the couturiers at the beginning of each season to determine a decorative theme, be it Etruscan, Renaissance or Provençal. Many styles and decorative details were revived, and for this reason records or prototype pieces of every pin, button or parure were filed away in the drawers of vast chests, to be copied.

Roger Scemama, who had worked with Schiaparelli in the 1930s and then suffered as a prisoner of war, was helped back on to his feet by Dior's patronage. He produced precious-looking costume jewelry by placing colourful Czechoslovakian stones into 'antique-style' settings, with the precision of a fine jeweler. Couture jewelry was justified, he claimed, by the fact that it offered women affordable change. 'Every day I take my dog for a walk down the street and sometimes I meet a woman who is exercising her dog too. She has a modern, gold necklet, which is very pretty, but I've never seen her without it. I can recognise her by that necklet in the distance. If she hadn't got it she would surely buy some artificial jewelry, and be able to change it more often.'

Opposite A treasure trove of imitation pearls, diamanté, crystal and rhinestones by Francis Winter, Gripoix and Henry à la Pensée, 1961. *William Klein*

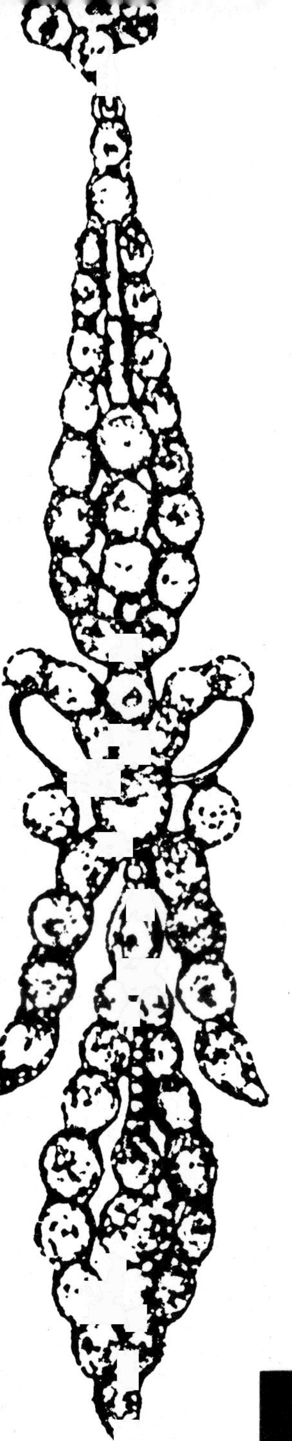

Earrings of the 1950s combined imitation and grandeur to set off the period's more feminine and formal clothing. Georgian paste, Victorian bows, or delicate Edwardian drops were all copied by contemporary costume jewelers.

Opposite Paste chandelier earrings and matching necklace, 1957. *Irving Penn*

Below Castlecliff's ornate pendant earrings with loveknots of brilliants, 1947

This page, right (from top to bottom) Castlecliff's pearl drop clip-ons, 1954, *Otto Maya*; Monet's gilt wheels-within-wheels, 1954, *Otto Maya*; Shreiner's tiny crystal and rhinestone stars, 1954, *Otto Maya*; Bogoff's large sunburst of rhinestones and fake tourmalines, 1959. *Evelyn Hofer*

Left Shoulder-length paste pendant earring, 1957

Below Earmuff-size rhinestone, fake pearl and fake emerald earrings by Marvella, 1959. *Evelyn Hofer*

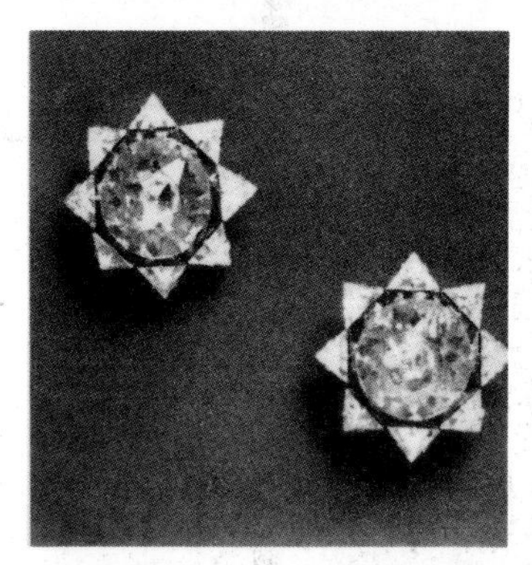

Bold gilt jewelry provided the luxurious and dramatic image craved by women during the 1940s and 1950s. Regardless of the colour or style of their clothes, gilt was compatible. However, to give the proper air of high drama and opulence it had to be heavy and well-gilded, often with two or three shades of gilding on one piece.

Main picture (along arms from left to right) Bubley's flexible gilt chain with cactus blossoms tipped with rhinestones; Nettie Rosenstein's gold-plated cuff bracelet worn with Miriam Haskell's two drop bracelets; Monet's triangular earrings. In the cleft of the shoulder, a rhinestone-tipped brooch and three solid upper arm bracelets by Castlecliff; Schiaparelli's twisted link bracelet with swinging tassels; Napier's thin double bangle, and, finally, Monet's three bangles worn with two furrowed link bracelets, 1953. *Erwin Blumenfeld*

Opposite, above Monet's triple decker gilt chain bracelets held together by a T-bar and worn with lacy gilt and topaz earrings, 1959. *Evelyn Hofer*

Below right Mosell's pair of gilt rope bracelets with multicoloured stones caught up in the twists, 1959. *Evelyn Hofer*

Centre Capri's bracelet of a thousand silvery wires tipped with rhinestones, 1954. *Otto Maya*

The big pin explosion – large, gem-encrusted spirals, comets and stars – brightened the simple, tailored day clothes of the early 1960s. Jacques Fath had popularized the fashion for wearing a constellation of exploding pins across the lapel a decade earlier.

Above A roundel of gilt leaves radiating from a large black stone, by Drega for Givenchy, 1961. *Willy Rizzo*

Centre left Noella Riotteau's intricate rosette pin of trellised gold and pink diamanté, 1961. *Willy Rizzo*

Centre right A spiral of black and yellow Tyrol stones curled into a pin, by Mayse Blanchard for Dior, 1961. *Willy Rizzo*

Left Dior's *bijoux* pin; a gilt wild duck with brilliants and gold wings, faux-ruby eyes and a faux-emerald neck, 1961. *Willy Rizzo*

Opposite Pin dripping with green stones, from Paris House, 1961. *Claude Virgin*

Imitation turquoise and pearl pin by Adrian Mann, 1961. *Claude Virgin*

In 1955 Dior approached Henkel and Grossé of Pforzheim to mass manufacture his exclusive range of seasonal fashion jewelry, so setting a precedent which many couturiers were to follow. The firm prided itself on its precision craftsmanship, on the fact that there was no conveyor belt, no mechanical assembly of parts. Handwork continued to be the most valuable ingredient of fine costume jewelry. Since nothing could be realized without knowledge of the production capabilities of the manufacturer, close collaboration by the designer was essential from the start. The fashion house also controlled the marketing and display of the jewels, for it was of course one aspect of the couturier's image that was being sold.

Department store retailing of costume jewelry was fiercely competitive. Leading manufacturers, such as Napier, Trifari, Monet and Corocraft, who competed with the couture house names, sold their jewelry like a cosmetic, each counter prominently displaying the manufacturer's name. Personal service, after-sales service and an attempt to maintain a personal contact with each customer were offered as attractions. Loss leader sales techniques were competitively employed to entice potential custom: free gifts, gifts with purchase and private consultations.

After First Lady Mamie Eisenhower chose to wear Trifari jewels to both her inaugural balls, copies of her pieces flooded the market and Trifari brought an action for breach of copyright. A legal precedent was set when the court ruled that the piece of costume jewelry in question was a work of art and therefore should be protected by an art copyright. Mrs Eisenhower's gesture, combined with this ruling, established the universal acceptability of costume jewelry. By the 1950s it had found its way into every woman's trinket box, alongside, although never entirely replacing, her fine jewelry.

Adrian Mann was one of the first costume jewelry wholesalers in London to attract a popular market. Before the war he had worked for Lyon Weill in Paris and had maintained contacts with several Czechoslovakian stone producers. Having settled in Britain after the war, he opened his own company. Despite the immediate postwar shortages, Mann was able to buy a stock of Czech pearls, greatly in demand, and sell them as earrings, buttons and brooches to the major department stores. Contracts followed with couture houses such as Hartnell and Amies and he soon realized that the costume jewelry market was extremely lucrative. Moving to the retail side of the business by taking a counter in various department stores, Mann pioneered the technique of selling jewelry as if it were a cosmetic, pouring investment and expertise into the packaging and advertising of a product of little intrinsic value. Novelty and fashion appropriateness were the guiding themes.

Opposite Roger Scemama's bold blue moth-ball pearls encircle the upstanding collar of Saint Laurent's silk suit, 1963. *William Klein*

OVERLEAF

Selection of jet jewelry, the key accessory of Saint Laurent's Winter 1962 collection. *Top* Coil necklace with clusters of gold and jet beads, echoed by bunches of jet and rhinestone in matching button earrings. *Centre* Thick plait of jet beads, studded with black pearls and amethysts. *Below left* Jet and ruby stone pendant suspended from a simple, unjewelled chain. *Below centre* Jagged stone earrings with jet metal backs, beside a jewelled and linked double crescent pin with attached pearls. *Below right* Anthracite heart-shaped pendant on a thin jewelled chain

Similarly Fried Frères in Paris began to retail as well as wholesale costume jewelry to a mass market, opening in 1956 their own boutique 'Bijoux Box' which offered a wide range of paste, glass, plastic and pearl trinkets. Albert Weiss founded his costume jewelry company in 1942, having worked at Corocraft, Marvella Jewelry and Grad & Schrager. He became noted for his enamel flower jewelry produced in the fifties.

Above Grey, white and black cut-crystal bead necklace from Dior, 1961. *Irving Penn*

Below Marvella's 'Poppet' necklace, 1964. *Bert Stern*

As the dollar weakened after the war and the cost of labour escalated in Europe, the American mass market producers began to manufacture their components in the Far East, particularly in Hong Kong and Korea. Output was increased by new methods of production, particularly centrifugal casting of metals and injection moulding of plastics – a cheaper method of manufacturing beads than blown glass. Specific towns were renowned for certain production processes. The perfection of stronger metal alloys and numerous acrylics increased the variety of materials available to the industry, and their relative cheapness effected a dramatic extension of the market. There was a shift from the more expensive casting to blanketing, in which sophisticated machinery could cut the pieces of metal from a block to the exact size while simultaneously adding pattern and texture.

Costly glass was replaced by plastic, thereby changing the look from imitation to bold and colourful junk. Fashion was, consequently, determined by production techniques. Gradually eighteenth-century-inspired paste was superseded by obviously cheap plastic, fun jewelry – such as colourful plastic bangles and beads.

'Poppets', one of the few pieces of junk jewelry known to almost everybody, are a superb example of how thoroughly a fad could sweep through the Western world. These pop-together plastic beads in various colours were invented and patented by Geoffrey Charles in 1953 and sold through Walter Scaife Ltd and Elizabeth Arden in London. Following an initial local success, Richelieu Pearls in America were approached to pearlize and market them. Everyone who was a child in the 1950s remembers the endless permutations of these cheap, versatile and popular beads.

Opposite Mimi de N's cuff bracelets with strands of tangled gilt, suspended with fake rubies and pearls, 1964. *Irving Penn*

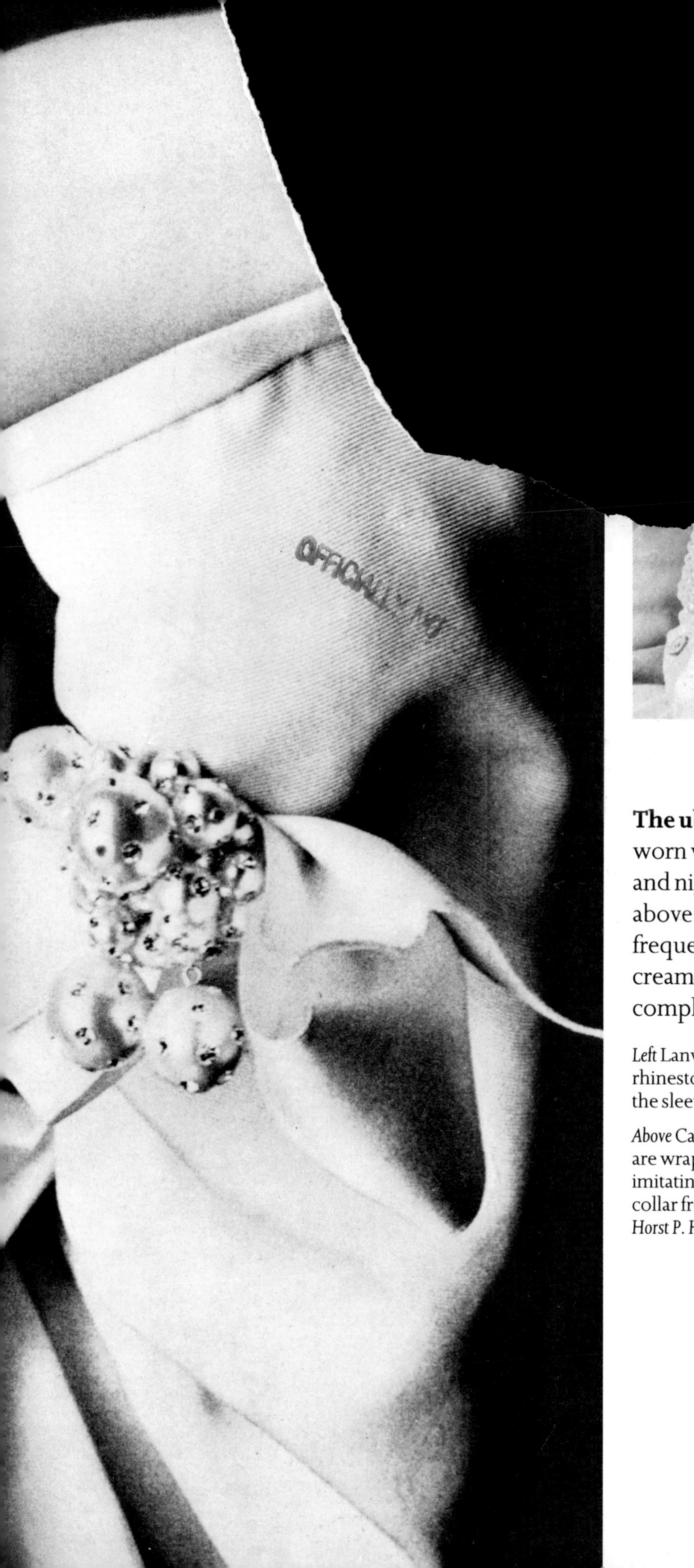

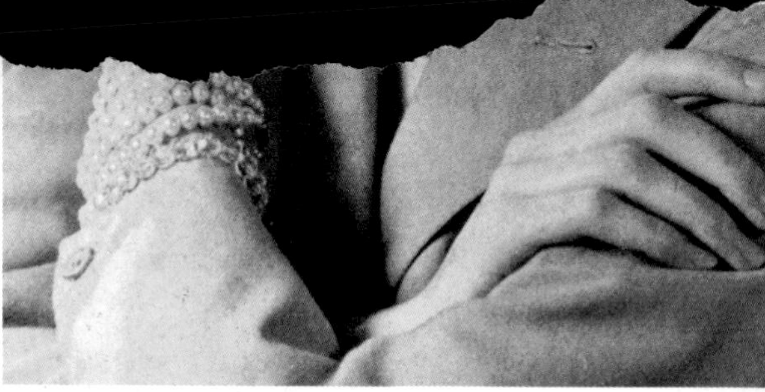

The ubiquitous pearl, like gilt, could be worn with most ensembles, by both day and night, being classic, adaptable and – above all – feminine. Pearl beads were frequently dyed – coffee, lemon yellow, cream or grey, for example – to complement the hue of an outfit.

Left Lanvin-Castillo's pearly baubled pin set with rhinestones, clipped to the ribbon on the outside of the sleeve, 1961. *Irving Penn*

Above Castlecliff's crystal and imitation pearl ropes are wrapped around a handkerchief at the neck, imitating Dior's revival of the Edwardian boned collar from his New Look collection, 1947. *Horst P. Horst*

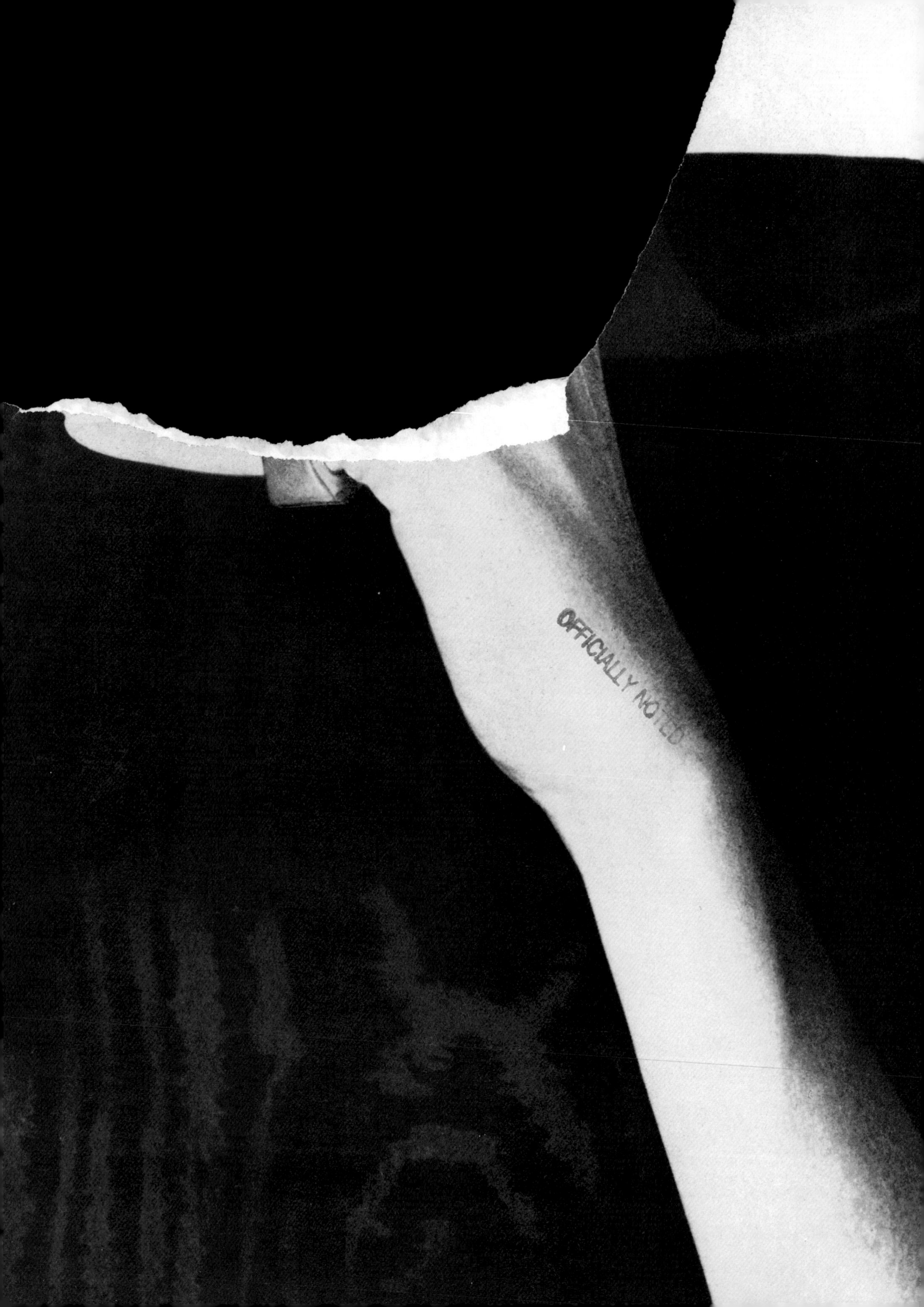
OFFICIALLY NOTED

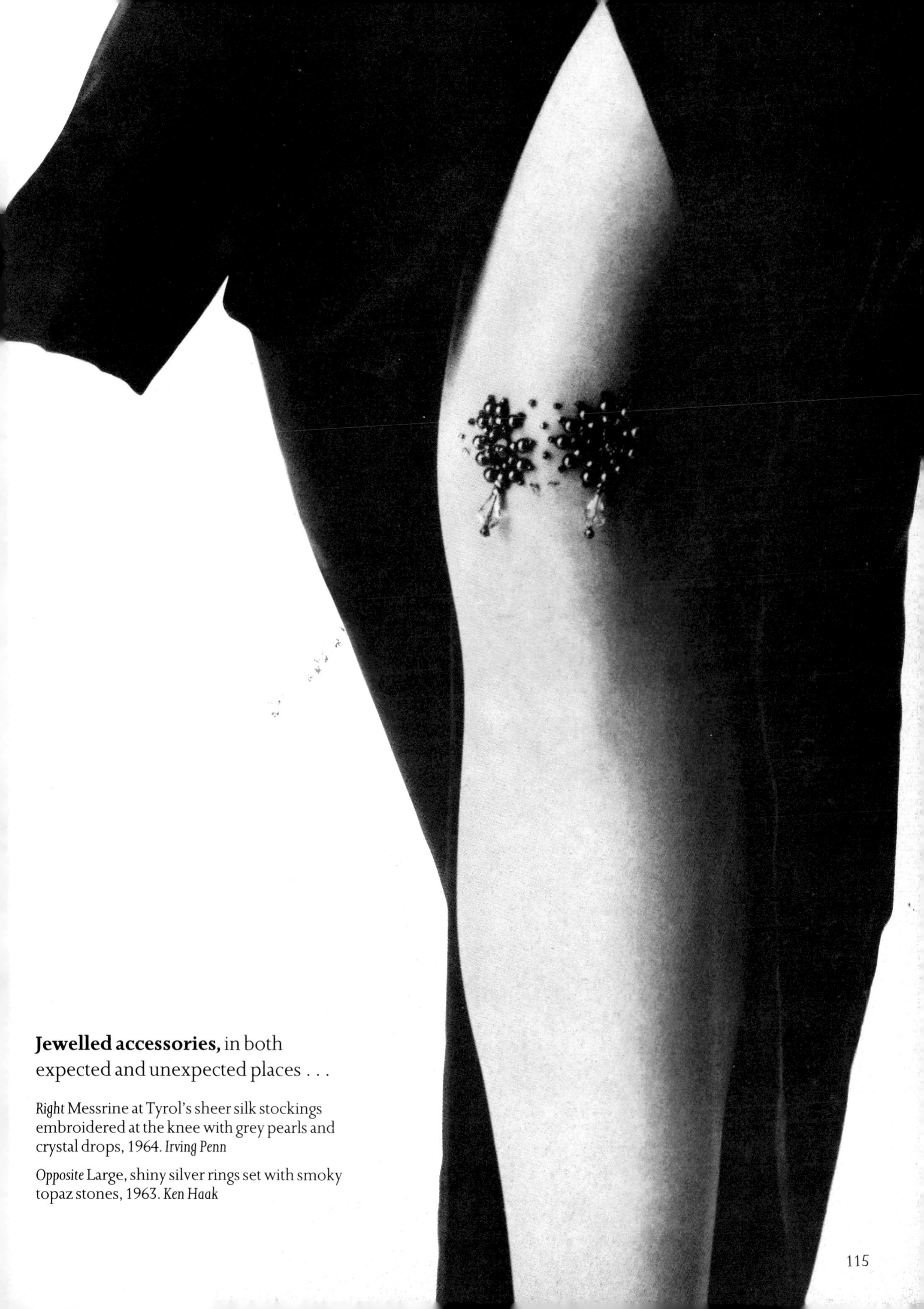

Jewelled accessories, in both expected and unexpected places . . .

Right Messrine at Tyrol's sheer silk stockings embroidered at the knee with grey pearls and crystal drops, 1964. *Irving Penn*

Opposite Large, shiny silver rings set with smoky topaz stones, 1963. *Ken Haak*

Jet jewelry threw off its association with mourning after the First World War. By the 1960s it had become the perfect complement to the simple, monochromatic clothing that prevailed in high fashion.

Far left Massed strands and beads of gleaming jet in a collar by Roger Jean Pierre for Saint Laurent, 1962. *Irving Penn*

Left Three slim chains of polished jet – linked and beaded – from Paris House, 1953. *Anthony Denney*

Above Givenchy's ornate drop jet earrings and matching jet-embroidered tulle cap, 1954. *Henry Clarke*

Below Victorian-style bonnet of fine black tulle, sparkling with jet and crowned with an ostrich feather, 1948. *Norman Parkinson*

Above Gabrielle Chanel, wearing a selection of her own jewelry, 1953. *Sabine Weiss*

Below Iridescent mauve cabochon stones set in a brooch created, probably by Gripoix, for Chanel, 1954. *Sabine Weiss*

Chanel's return in 1954 from semi-retirement was of paramount importance in highlighting the use of costume jewelry in high fashion. Her postwar look was based on an exaggeration of the earlier, quintessential Chanel style. It was during this period that the multi-layers of gilt, glass stones and pearls became associated internationally with the house of Chanel. She was fortunate enough to work with one of the leading craftsmen of her day, M. Goossens. He recalls that Chanel could judge the final look of a suit or dress only when it was accompanied by its jewels. In her eyes the first was naked without the second. Balenciaga, on the other hand, had only a modest respect for costume jewelry and thought that the effect of a well-cut dress should be entirely independent of superficial decoration. As the master of precise cut, he considered the unadorned, sculptural lines of a dress to be far more important than the dazzling trinkets added as an afterthought. If embellishment were needed, he preferred encrusted embroidery.

Goossens fashioned a variety of styles for his different clients: gilt and pearl work for Chanel, colourful beadwork and strass for Balenciaga. He regarded himself as an interpreter rather than a creator. Having determined a theme with Chanel, for example, for a collection based on thirteenth-century religious motifs, he would return with prototypes styled as necklaces. Chanel would immediately reinterpret them as belts and so the creative process evolved. A similar process is apparent time and time again in the history of costume jewelry and leads one to the conclusion that couturiers can by no means take all the credit for costume jewelry designs.

Goossens was not born into the costume jewelry craft but worked in his father's atelier making *objets d'art*, such as little brass and bronze souvenir statues. Here he learnt the skills of gilding and casting, and in 1952 was approached by Chanel to make jewelry. In common with many others, he found Chanel exceedingly difficult to work with, though he respected her for her demanding nature and her contempt for the amateur, which drove her to extract the highest standards of workmanship from colleagues.

By the mid-fifties the market for costume jewelry had expanded for several reasons: high fashion's imprimatur, the mass production of attractive pieces and the new fashion-consciousness of the less wealthy who, while they could ill-afford real gems, demanded amusing and decorative accessories to their clothes.

In 1954 May V. Clark, a market researcher working for a British firm, prepared a report on the US costume jewelry market. She pointed out that the American tenet of 'Buy new, discard the old' produced an ideal market in which to sell novelty pieces covering a wide price range which could be bought as gifts and which would add sparkle to classic clothes. 'Conversation piece' jewelry was particularly popular with American women: various

Opposite left Jean Shrimpton wears an armload of multicoloured poppy-seed bangles, 1964. *David Bailey*

Right Shirley MacLaine, in the style of the Nancy Cunard pose of the 1920s, wears a stack of Van S's wooden and Lucite bangles, 1964. *Bert Stern*

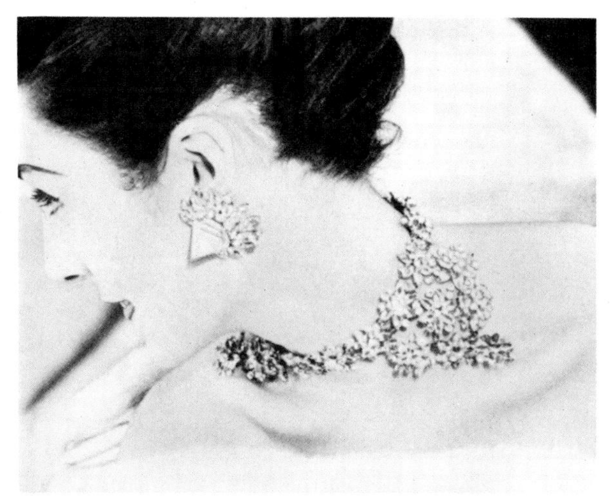

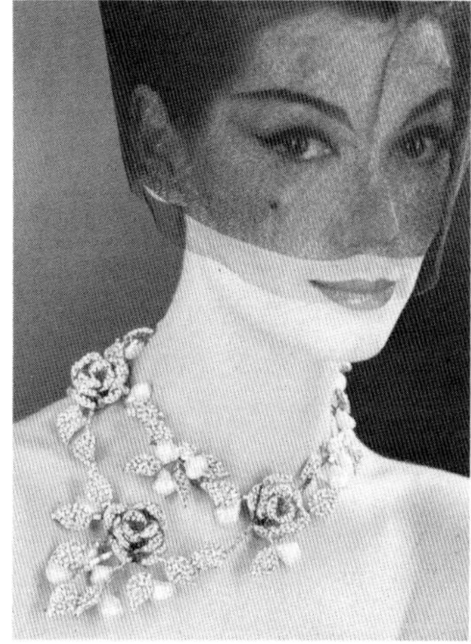

Above left Fath's ermine stole worn with an asymmetrical, strass collier and strass and mother-of-pearl earrings, 1954. *Henry Clarke*

Above right Asymmetrical jewelry – Gripoix's rhinestone and pearl, roses and leaves necklace for Givenchy's Autumn 1957 collection. *Henry Clarke*

coloured artificial eye rings and pins, storks holding babies, or the 'Faith charm' – a grain of mustard seed in a glass globe.

Big manufacturers, such as Trifari, sent designers to the European dress shows every season to coordinate a fashionable look. According to May V. Clark, houses such as Trifari created three independent lines: tailored plastic and 'gold' jewelry; dress jewelry, with stones and enamel to match the season's fashion colours; and items that imitated fine jewelry. She estimated that the turnover of the entire fashion jewelry trade in the United States came to 500 million dollars a year.

The partnership between clothes and jewelry was confirmed by the work of designers such as Eisenberg in America. Beginning before the war, he soon found that the trinkets he designed to accompany his outfits proved more popular than the clothes themselves. He set about specializing in costume jewelry and created the most collectable pieces of the late fifties.

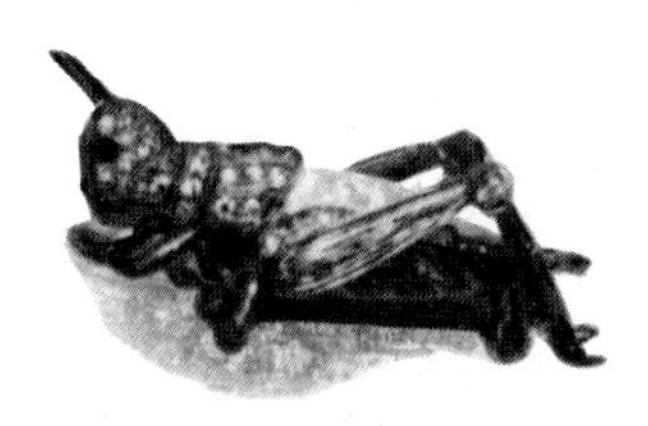

White porcelain and gold-plated grasshopper brooch from Saks Fifth Avenue, 1959

In *Lady Behave*, a guide to modern manners written in 1956 by Anne Edwards and Drusilla Beyfus, the snobbish attitude towards fake jewelry was finally debunked. 'At a time when people with real jewelry spoke disparagingly of "imitations", these imitations were cheap replicas of the originals – paste clips which were copies of the real diamond kind... rabbit skins which were marked to look like mink, and art silk made to simulate real silk. Today there is a new fashion for fakes, which no one could disparage, because the fakes have a distinctive elegance of their own.' Fashionable women quite happily put on Parisian glass and rhinestone jewels, nylon stockings, fake fun furs and colourful synthetics, and others followed suit, though the authors expressed regret that there 'always will be those with little sense of fashion who think it better to wear a fox in diamond chips because it is genuine, rather than an elegant Parisian fake'. These women still exist today.

By the end of the fifties, *Vogue* had identified a 'bright-bead craze', necks wrapped high with beads encased with gold filigree work. Beads and baubles had replaced cut-glass stones. Alison Adburgham observed in a 1960

Opposite Multicoloured rows of over-sized, *papier-mâché* beads, painted and glazed by Arpad, 1964. *Bert Stern*

issue of *Punch* that 'the coming cult is evident in jewelry that is more chunky, less glittery, with a strong tendency to medallions, chains, and ropes of amber. Necklaces knot instead of clasping, and drop-earrings significantly disappear.'

Tailored blouses sported cufflinks of gilt, or gilt and stones, and French *Vogue* declared 'Le pacte Jersey-Bijoux' in 1957: twinsets were loaded down with brightly coloured beads, and wrists weighted with strings of baubles and slave bangles.

A change in popular taste was evident in the early 1960s. More and more young women had disposable income and tore free from the sartorial guidelines of their mothers. To these teenagers novelty and innovation were more highly prized than imitation. They designed and demanded costume jewelry to make them laugh, denote a political or social stance and proclaim their modernity. The introduction of new materials and novel shapes changed the popular concepts of costume jewelry.

Left Marella Agnelli's inimitable style: silk shirt, Capri pants and a throat-load of coloured beads, 1957. *René Bouché*

Opposite left Arpad's perfect foil for a backless dress – a cascade of crystal, rhinestone and faux-emeralds and matching earrings, 1958. *Clifford Coffin*

Right An extra-long rope of liquorice and white beads, 1961. *Eugène Vernier*

Gripoix continued to design ornate, stone-set gilt jewelry for Chanel when the latter reopened her house in 1954. The typical multicoloured, cabochon stone and *pâte de verre* elements, inspired by Renaissance jewelry and the Romanov collection, once more entered high fashion, to be copied in turn by mass-producers.

Opposite Roger Jean Pierre's wide, gold-mesh collar studded with rhinestones and pearl flowers and worn with matching flower clips, 1962. *Brian Duffy*

This page Big beautiful bravura jewels made by Gripoix for Chanel

Above Bold rope necklace of imitation pearls and emeralds with a large sunburst pin of ruby and rhinestone, 1956. *William Grigsby*

Below Gilt coil necklace with intertwined imitation sapphires and emeralds in its chain and pendant cluster, 1956. *William Grigsby*

Couture jewels complement the perfect tailored simplicity that is the hallmark of the *grandes maisons*. Couture clothes are given the finishing touch by the addition of a single, distinctive piece of thematic jewelry, invariably of limited edition. Saint Laurent was the most consistent promoter of original costume jewelry; each collection was accessorized by a new range. By contrast, Balenciaga was circumspect; jewelry, he believed, might detract from the beauty of a simple yet masterful silhouette – he used it sparingly, as did his *protégé* Courrèges.

Opposite, left Saint Laurent's mink-cuffed black jacket sheath dress and velvet hat and Coppola and Toppo's collier for Saint Laurent, 1962, from the designer's first collection

Above Rich green stone pendant on a gilt chain adds a Renaissance detail to Balenciaga's tweed day suit, 1962. *William Klein*

This page, below Mosaic plaques of amethyst, yellow, green and ruby stones decorate Capucci's piqué tea gown, 1963. *Karen Radkai*

Right A dramatic counterpoint to Courrèges' all-white ensemble: Jeanne Péral's glistening black pendant on a heavy rope, 1964. *William Klein*

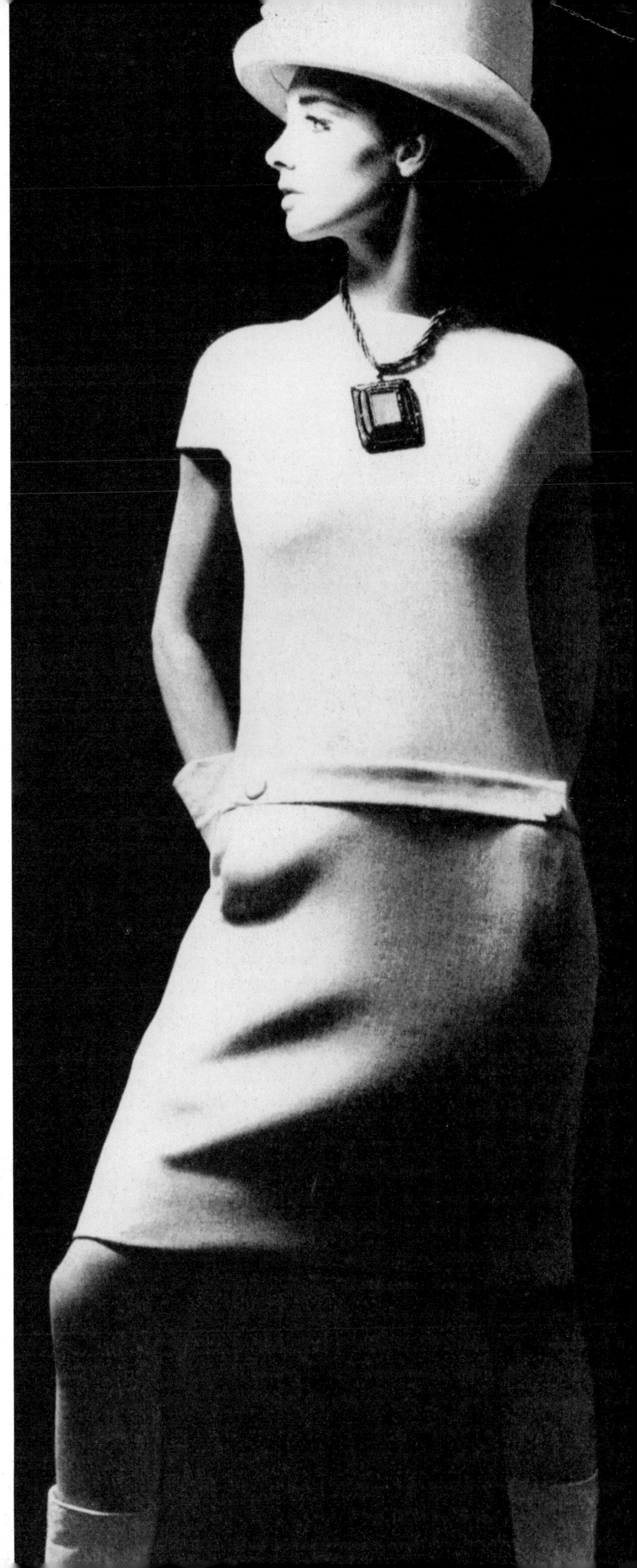

4 · 1965–1987

Brash Fakery, Creative Salvage, Couture Jewels Revived

'In 1963 I invented costume jewelry for the beautiful people – was lionized by them and became one of the most splendidly beautiful of them – a genuine sixties character! Handsome, tall, thin… sitting in the back of my vintage Rolls (with matching driver) wearing either my floor-length leopard – or monkey – or unicorn coat – all of which have disappeared.' So recalled Ken Lane, the designer who dominated the costume jewelry market in the mid-1960s and who was one of the most flamboyant contributors to the New York fashion scene.

Lane knew nothing about jewelry-making techniques. He had been designing shoes for Delman, Dior and Roger Vivier and simply began to experiment with the materials he had been using for decoration, such as leather and diamanté. He made dangling earrings by taking cotton wool balls normally used as Christmas tree decorations and covering them with sequins. Inspired by Victorian snake bracelets, he wrapped wooden or plastic bangles with cobra skins.

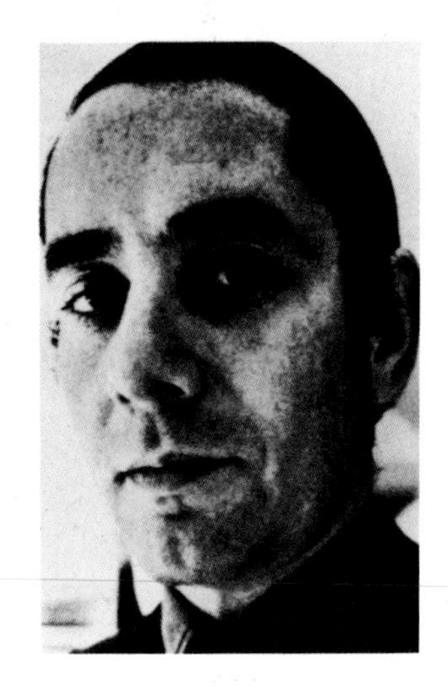

Above Ken Lane, 1969. *Stefan Tyszko*

Opposite Maurice Jacob's red-white-and-blue sequinned ball bracelet, ring and earrings, 1968. *Bert Stern*

Lane also enamelled shells to make into jewelry; 'You've no idea how long it takes to find two sea snail shells alike enough for a pair of earrings.' His pink and black or mock-lapis lazuli and black plastic rings, dress clips and bangles, all in the Art Deco style; his diamanté-encrusted enamel animal bangles; and his copies of Bulgari and Cartier jewelry became fashion classics.

In the 1950s, Marella Agnelli had popularized the wearing of rows and rows of fake and real spherical beads; not strung between gilt links and hanging down the front of an ensemble, in the Chanel style, but strung simply and worn close to the throat. In imitation, Ken Lane prompted fashionable women to don throat-loads of his spherical baubles. In 1966 he was presented with the Coty Award, fashion's equivalent of an Oscar, for popularizing these grandly gaudy ephemera.

Diana Vreeland, editor-in-chief of American *Vogue*, featured 'K.J.L.' novelties constantly: pearl rings the size of golf balls, 'gobstopper' earrings, fake-marble plastic bangles, mock-*pâte-de-verre* parures, mock-Lalique and

Above left Ken Lane's plaited pearl bead ponytail and Apex Art's rhinestone cluster ring, 1965.
Gordon Parks

Above Wendy Gells's 'wristys' and Eric Beamon's beaded ponytail, 1986.
Irving Penn

imitation-Indian jewelry and black eyeball earrings and rings with diamanté centres. On his travels, Lane would collect souvenirs, such as Viennese or Indian bronze figures, the heads of which he cast in plastic or gilded metal for brooches and knuckle-duster rings. Wit and irreverence were to him the touchstones of good costume jewelry and he admitted that he 'had a lot of fun before I got serious.' 'Oh, when was that?' 'Tomorrow, tomorrow!'

Fellow-American Giorgio di Sant'Angelo mastered *the* fashionable sixties material: plastic. In 1964, having worked as a Walt Disney animator and an architect, he began experimenting with plastic sculptures. Du Pont, the synthetic material manufacturers, suggested that he promote plastic in the fashion world. The geometric jewelry that he designed in this material dominated an entire issue of American *Vogue*. From then on, he was regularly commissioned to accessorize *Vogue*'s pages. His witty novelties included embedding real diamonds in clear plastic balls or encasing the fashion model Veruschka's painted body with gold wire and coloured curtain cords hung with roughly hewn stones.

In the mid-1960s, Diana Vreeland observed that chain jewelry had completely slipped from fashion and that its manufacturers were struggling to stay in business. She approached di Sant'Angelo with the idea that he should promote it. With a trunk load of cloth, ribbon, stones and trinkets, he left for the Arizona desert, taking with him Veruschka and the photographer Franco Rubartelli. Back came some of the most alluring pictures of the era, encouraging a fad for chainmail bikinis, chain swags across bellies and a range of chain beachwear jewelry, which had everything to do with avant-garde fashion but very little with the clothing industry.

Opposite Ken Lane's multicoloured, beaded bracelets with enamel and stone clasps, 1965.
Irving Penn

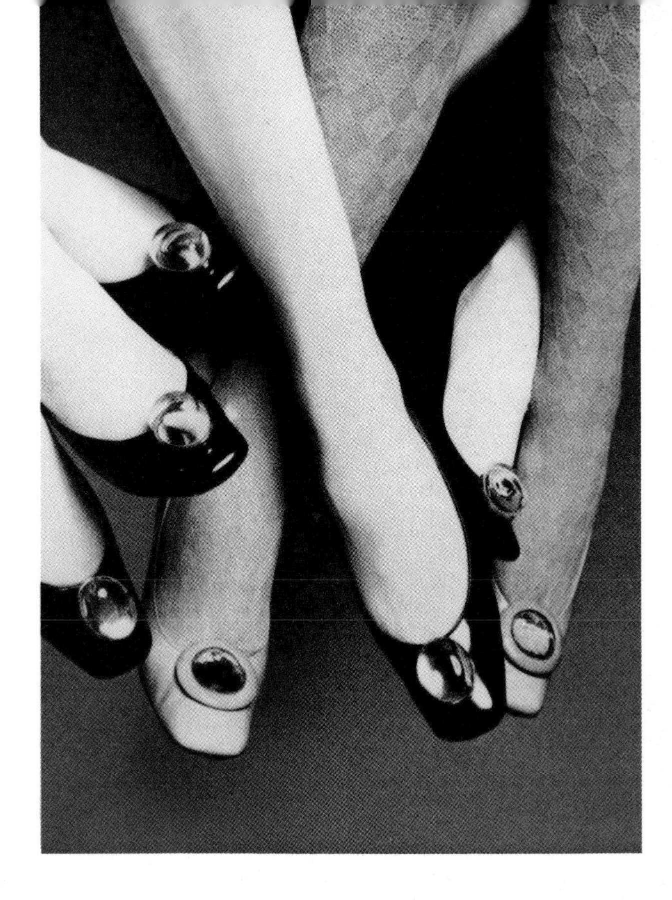

Left Shoes with decorative Perspex discs by Charles Jourdan, 1967. *Guy Bourdin*

Right Arline Fisch's (for Lee Nordess Gallery) chased silver body sculpture – a panel of metal hung with chiming tears, 1969. *Alexis Waldeck*

Opposite Op-Art-inspired black and white ear- and finger-rings by Ingeborg/Georgio for Richelieu, 1966. *Franco Rubartelli*

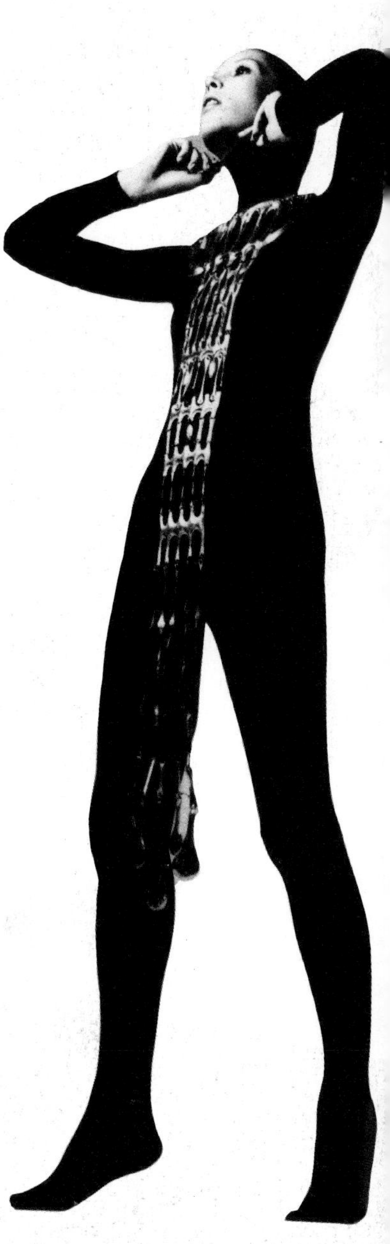

Di Sant'Angelo brought costume jewelry to new heights because he saw it not simply as jewelry, but as body decoration, for which he took his inspiration from the body adornment of primitive peoples. Costume jewelry now 'clothed' the body, with chainmail vests and breastplates being worn in lieu of clothing.

The childlike simplicity of the mid-sixties shift was enhanced by plain, geometric jewelry. Bold, clear black-and-white constructions in plastic, Perspex and dyed woods also reflected contemporary interest in the Op Art of Bridget Riley and Paule Vézélay and the plexiglass sculpture of Eric Olsen and Francisco Sobrino.

The fascination with man-made materials, particularly moulded plastics, plexiglass (I.C.I. Perspex) and vinyl, was a prominent characteristic of mid-sixties fashion. Perspex had been introduced during the Second World War and used for the canopies of fighter planes. Airmen would bend fragments of the material over heat to make trinkets for their girlfriends. In 1966 Paco Rabanne began stamping the material into chainmail shapes while Charles Jourdan cut ice-cube-shaped Perspex heels and decorations on his shoes. Numerous designers offered jewelry cut from laminated sheets of acrylic.

Wendy Ramshaw in London designed the most fashionable Perspex and paper jewelry, working with her cousin, Patricia Howard, under the name 'Something Special'. She screen-printed and then cut and hand polished Perspex to accessorize the black and white Mod and geometric fashions of the period. But this jewelry brought Ramshaw little commercial success since the market was soon flooded with copies.

Body sculpture looked its best against bare flesh or simple, unpatterned clothing. As the boundaries of conventional jewelry were extended, it could be worn on those parts of the body that tribal jewelry had never disregarded.

Opposite Mimi de N's silvery breastplate and Sol Kass for Mark XIV's chrome finger-sheaths, 1969. *Irving Penn*

Above Pablo and Delia's fluid silver leather coils, curving round the shoulder and across the forehead, 1970. *Clive Arrowsmith*

Right Silvano Malta's twisted blue cotton necklaces with silver rings, worn with a solid silver neck cuff, 1970

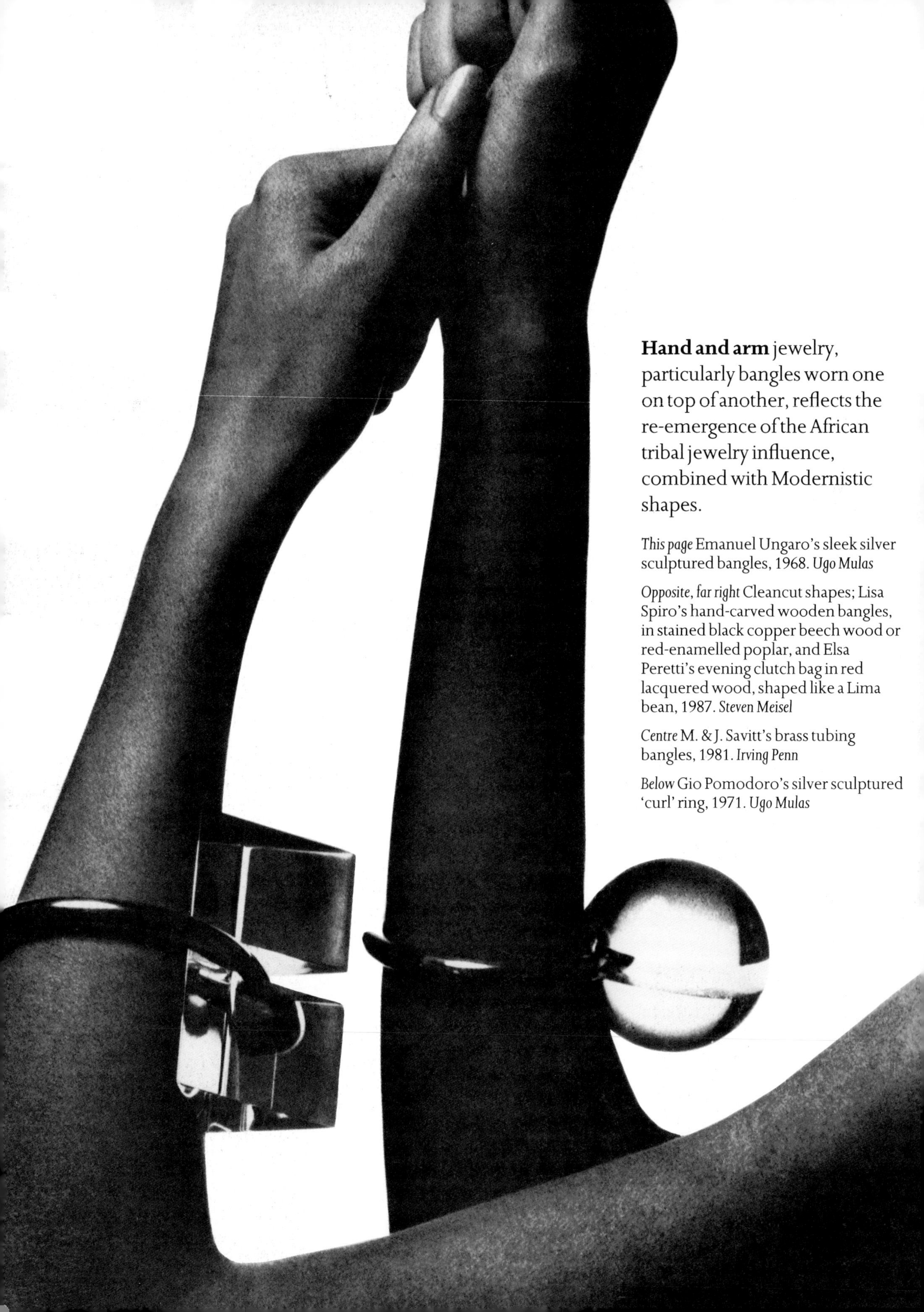

Hand and arm jewelry, particularly bangles worn one on top of another, reflects the re-emergence of the African tribal jewelry influence, combined with Modernistic shapes.

This page Emanuel Ungaro's sleek silver sculptured bangles, 1968. *Ugo Mulas*

Opposite, far right Cleancut shapes; Lisa Spiro's hand-carved wooden bangles, in stained black copper beech wood or red-enamelled poplar, and Elsa Peretti's evening clutch bag in red lacquered wood, shaped like a Lima bean, 1987. *Steven Meisel*

Centre M. & J. Savitt's brass tubing bangles, 1981. *Irving Penn*

Below Gio Pomodoro's silver sculptured 'curl' ring, 1971. *Ugo Mulas*

Her disposable paper jewelry of 1965 was cheap, versatile and novel. Flat paper-jewelry kits could be kept in a handbag and the jewelry made on the spot by folding perforated paper into a three-dimensional origami construction. The paper was printed with sixties ephemera – 'I'm Helping Britain' Union Jacks, psychedelia or day-glo. Paper butterflies complete with adhesive strips could be stuck to the skin or clothing. As paper is virtually weightless, Ramshaw was free to design jewelry as large as she liked to accessorize paper clothes. By 1966 there was a paper fashion boom, and symptomatic of this was the Paper Ball at the Wadsworth Atheneum Museum in Hartford, Connecticut, where all the guests wore paper dresses and even paper shoes.

It was Ramshaw, and other young British designers of the mid-sixties, such as David Watkins and Caroline Broadhead, who pioneered abstract ideas in jewelry. Rebelling against traditional notions, they promoted purely conceptual pieces which were difficult and even cumbersome to wear but which had a tremendous influence on the fashion jewelry market. 'A person doesn't need decoration; an attire may need some, but not a person,' stated the American jewelry designer Haikki M. Seppa, 'Decoration be damned! Beauty be damned! The refinement of ideas – either the maker's or the onlooker's (it doesn't matter which) – should be the purpose of jewelry.' Conceptual jewelry had arrived.

Modernism was soon overshadowed by eclecticism and nostalgia in high fashion. The antique mahogany counters of Biba, London's hippest fashion emporium, were covered with baskets overflowing with tat jewelry: coloured plastic, 'flapper' beads, Roman coin rings, plastic flower brooches, mock-Deco pins and bangles.

Below left Wendy Ramshaw's paper butterfly ring made from a do-it-yourself kit, 1967

Below right Net and satin skull-cap decorated with pearl beads, 1974. *Carlo Orsi*

Opposite Veruschka, dressed as a nomad in the Arizona desert, with Giorgio di Sant' Angelo's jewelry – stones wrapped in ropes, 1968. *Franco Rubartelli*

OVERLEAF

Left page Jean-Claude de Luca's amorphous-shaped plastic and Perspex combs. Triangular clasp at the end of the plait by Manfred Muller, 1980. *Yvonne Kranz*

Right page, above A variety of Prado's silver, amber and tortoise-shell combs and clasps embedded in tousled hair, 1986. *Albert Watson*

Below left Gio Pomodoro's silver and diamanté, lightning streak hair clasps, 1971. *Barry Lategan*

Below centre Pablo and Delia's round, painted-leather hair ornament, inspired by folk art, and held in place by a long pin, 1971. *Barry Lategan*

Below right Zandra Rhodes's sequin- and star-encrusted top hat and Mick Milligan's lightning 'gold' earrings, 1973. *David Bailey*

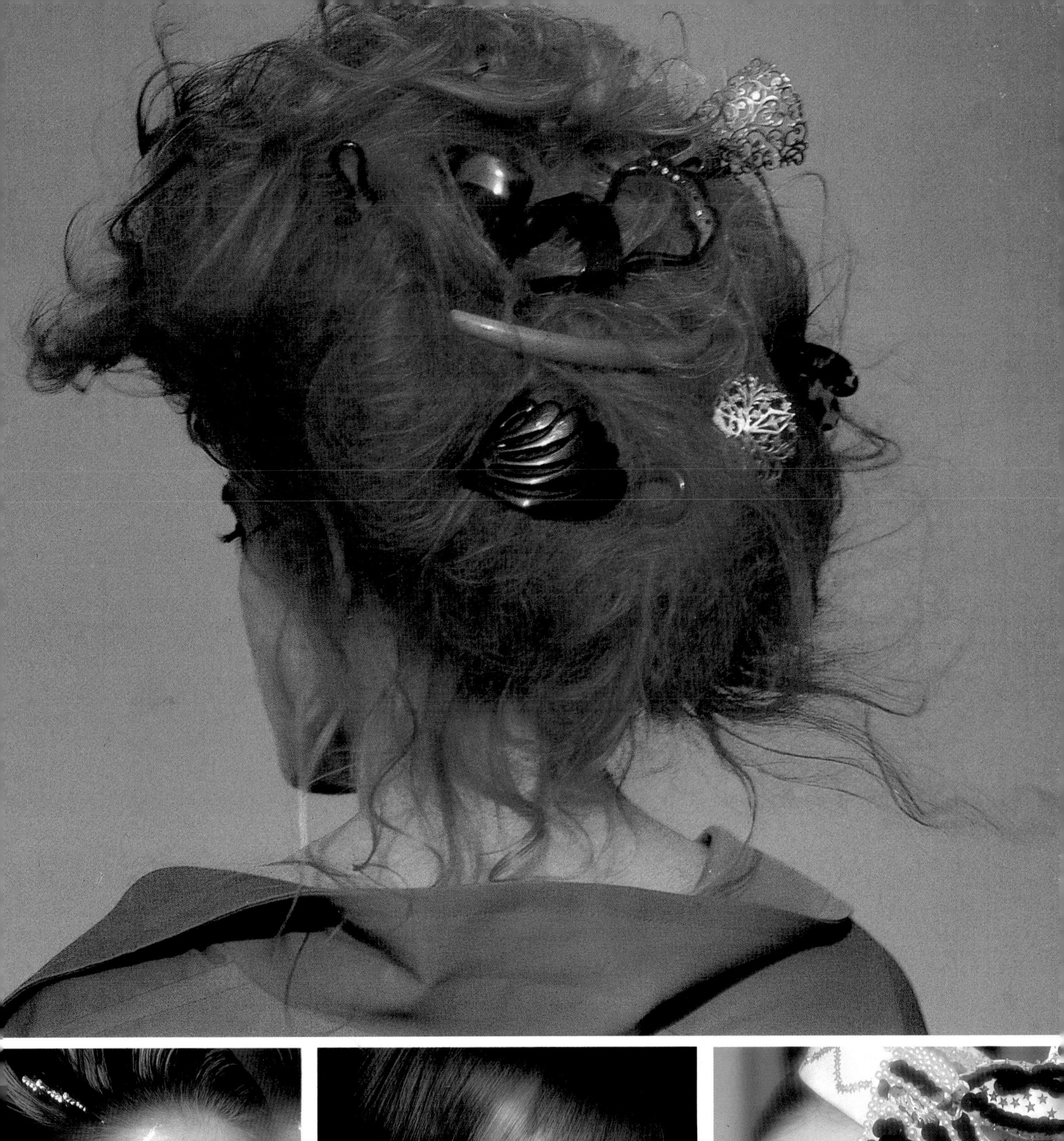

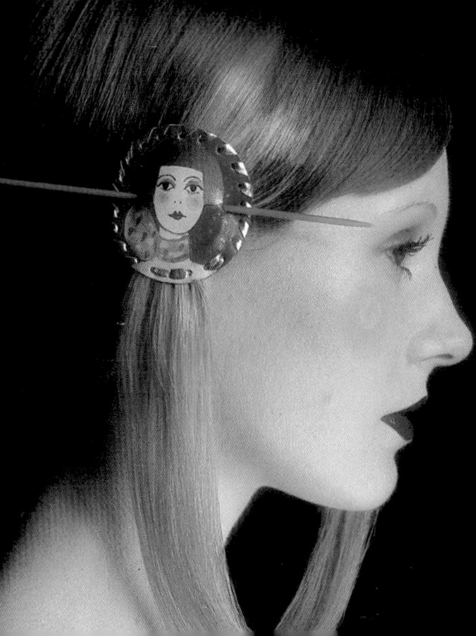

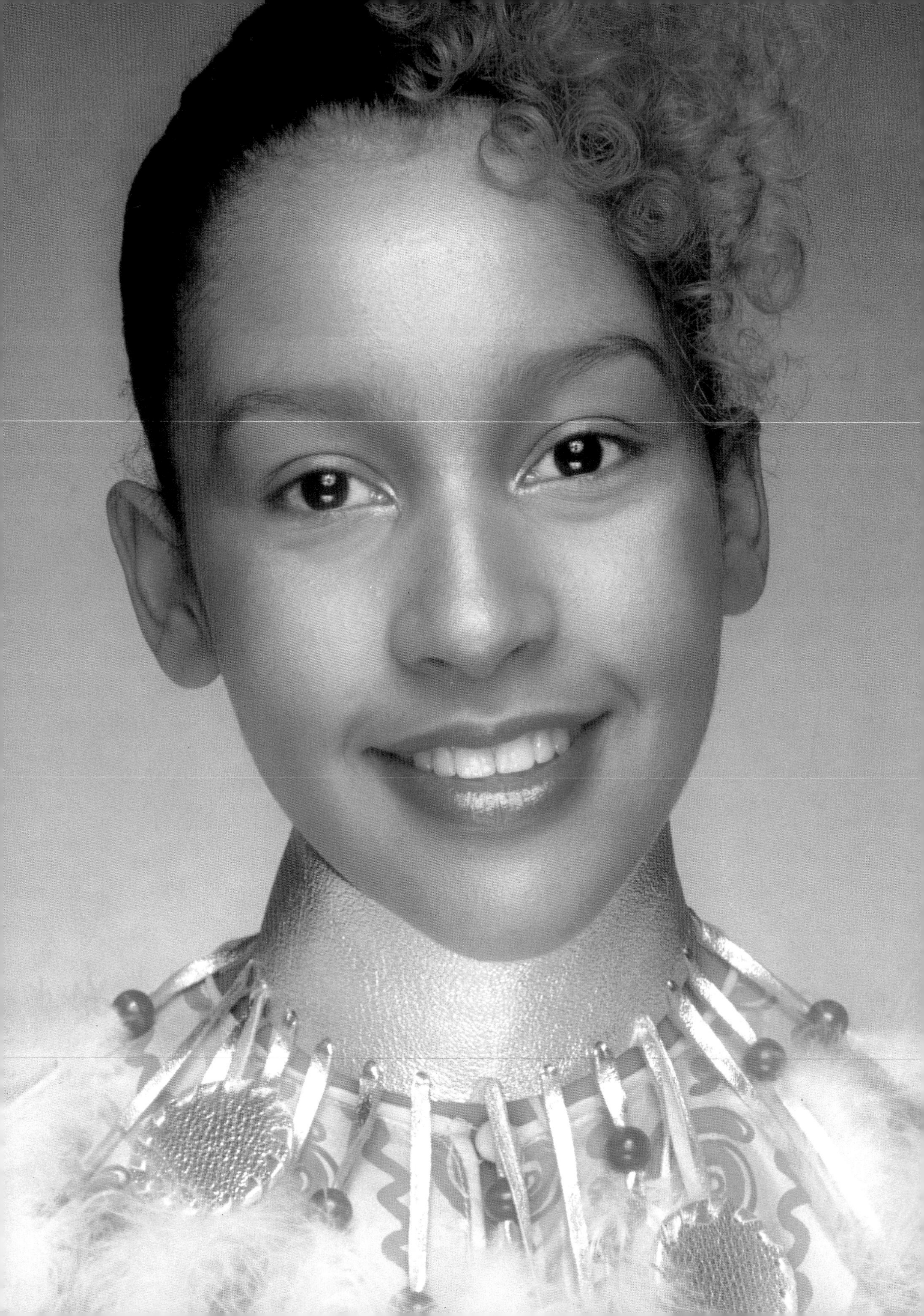

Niki de Saint Phalle's Surrealist necklace, 1974. *Carlo Orsi*

Eclectic references were sought by jewelry designers. By the late 1960s, for example, Pop Art themes were reproduced on costume jewelry. Mick Milligan in London presented witty interpretations of chrome and diamanté popular images for the London boutique Mr Freedom, such as Mickey Mouse badges, Disney bows, sailboats and cigarette-butt pins. His amusing prose jewelry, exemplified in a necklace studded with diamanté which read 'Diamonds are a girl's best friend', was very successful.

Various exhibitions, including one of Salvador Dali's jewelry in 1971 at The Whitechapel Gallery, London, and articles, such as George Melly's commentary in British *Vogue* on the merits of Surrealism, brought the designers' and public's attention to Surrealist themes. Fashion and costume jewelry designers began to experiment in this area.

Milligan was regularly commissioned by Zandra Rhodes to accessorize her collections, including her degree show at the Royal College of Art in 1967, for which he designed chrome and diamanté buttons. 'I work in three dimensions from Zandra's two-dimension fashion designs, in this case one of her strongest motifs – the lily.' He twisted and pleated gold-plated nickel and silver into lily headdresses and chokers for her Lily collection of 1972 and designed arrows for the Cactus Cowboy collection of that year, shells for her neo-crinolines in 1973 and abstracts in the late 1970s. By the early 1980s Andrew Logan and Valerie Robertson were also designing jewelry for Rhodes. Logan's resin shapes were embedded with smashed, multi-coloured glass and cut stones – the shapes varying according to the collection themes. Logan and Rhodes's travels through India inspired an Indian collection in 1985 for which Logan created jewelled turbans, Dali-like evil eyes and comma-shaped jewelry which echoed the shapes of the classic Indian paisley print. Pink, referred to by Diana Vreeland as the 'navy-blue of India', predominated in both the fabrics and accessories of this collection.

Below left Mick Milligan and Zandra Rhodes. Zandra Rhodes wears Milligan's prose necklace: 'Diamonds are a girl's best friend.' 1972. *Marit Lieberson*

Below right Andrew Logan, wearing two of his brooches, 1986. *Daffyd Jones*

Opposite Back to nature: long, colourfully streaked tresses held round the neck by a gilt and green bead butterfly pendant, 1969. *Barry Lategan*

PRECEDING PAGES

Left Marsha Hunt wears Pablo and Delia's wide silver leather neckband with silver thongs, blue beads and white feather, 1971. *Barry Lategan*

Right Tom Binns's skeletal wood and metal necklace, 1985. *Patrick Demarchelier*

Left A hippy couple wearing Woodstock-style headband watches; his of octagonal rhinestone and lapis lazuli by Omega, hers by Rolex, 1970. *Barry Lategan*

Above Manfredi's 'Love Beads' in delicate strands of amethyst and lapis lazuli, 1972. *Bugat*

Opposite Necklaces of boar's tusks worn with silver and ancient lumps of coral, and an ivory carved bracelet; elephant-hair rings and bracelet, 1969. *Clive Arrowsmith*

The routes followed by hippy travellers in the mid- and late-1960s opened many eyes to the magnificence of natural materials, such as African string jewelry hung with wood, bone and ivory and ornate Indian filigree pieces – perfect foils for ethnic kaftans and djellabahs. The young returned laden with an eclectic assortment that influenced jewelers in the West who, in turn, mass-produced or imported interlocking Greek puzzle rings, leather thongs, love beads and anklets. Many hippies and flower children who rejected conventional lifestyles turned to handicrafts as an alternative means of making a living. Pablo and Delia's leather thong jewelry hung with dyed feathers and wooden beads typified the ethnic style of the period.

Left Clare Murray's stiff, golden wire necklace and Paul Preston's fine gold flower chain round forehead, 1973. *Barry Lategan*

After the frivolity of sixties costume jewelry, there was an inevitable reaction against synthetics and Modernism in favour of natural materials and nostalgia. As women took to wearing fashion classics in natural materials – silk, cotton and wool – and retro clothing, so they accessorized these clothes with antique jewelry and hand-crafted, natural material jewelry. Arthur Rackham-style fairy pendants, Art Nouveau-style pieces and Art Deco jewelry became fashionable. Antique jewelry dealers promoted early twentieth-century paste, Bakelite and jet jewelry.

Nicki Butler and Simon Wilson, dealers in antique costume jewelry, were instrumental in encouraging the appreciation of costume jewelry, notably pieces from the early twentieth century. They started trading in Art Deco marcasite, paste and Bakelite in the late sixties in London and then restrung old pieces of French glass jewelry, such as flowers and beads, to create novel necklaces and bracelets. Original Bakelite pieces they etched with fashionable Pierrot figures. Their style was adopted by Grace Coddington, fashion editor on British *Vogue*, who encouraged her readers to collect and wear eye-catching, early-twentieth-century costume jewelry, which had been out of fashion for some time. From 1980, Butler and Wilson began designing their own costume jewelry collections.

Similarly, in the early seventies, Michel Lanz of Premier Etage started collecting old glass buttons, glass beads and shell buttons from the Parisian markets to make into retro jewelry. He was attracted by the instant gratification of making costume jewelry: the time between the conception of an idea and creation of the object was very short. Lanz subsequently designed jewelry for Saint Laurent, Mugler, Montana and Hanae Mori in a range of materials, notably geometric-shaped plastics.

Opposite Jet and marcasite rings and bangles from Butler and Wilson and Antiquarius, 1973. *Barry Lategan*

Gilt chain accessories had re-entered high fashion by the late 1960s to accompany the classic look promoted by Saint Laurent and Marc Bohan at Dior. Tailored city attire was accessorized by gilt chain necklaces or bracelets, handbags suspended from gilt chains and chain-link belts – smart, inoffensive accessories that were favoured by the executive woman, the *jolie madame* and the Preppie/Sloane Ranger.

Main picture From left to right: over the shoulder, a long fine chain of jet and gilt; around the neck, three chain belts by Paul Stephens. Finally, a slender, gold-plated chain and necklace of tiny gilt links and coloured stones, 1967. *Peter Rand*

Right Gilt chains with multicoloured stones with a belt of silver and gilt by Loris Abate for Mila Schön, 1971. *Oliviero Toscani*

Right Baroque necklace and earrings of filigree scrollwork of tiny seed pearls, worn with Thea Porter's ivory cotton brocade dress, 1971. *Barry Lategan*

Opposite Jean Shrimpton wears Milligan's aluminium choker, folded into a bow and gilded, 1974. *David Bailey*

OVERLEAF

Left page Enormous, glossy red, white and blue plastic bangles by Joia of New York, 1971

Right page Ferre's plastic, heart-shaped locket; on one side red enamel, on the other a sparkle of brilliants, 1971. *Alea Castaldi*

Centre Sports theme enamel badges, to be worn several at a time; sailing and tennis motifs by Point Rouge, the hockey motif by Cose, 1971. *Chris von Wangenheim*

Below left Missoni's Perspex 'knuckleduster' ring and brooch, of brightly coloured plastic flowers, 1973. *Gianni Penati*

Below right Pellini's shiny, geometric bead necklace in bubble-gum colours, 1986. *Tohru Nakamura*

FOLLOWING PAGES

Left page Butler and Wilson's 1930s-inspired chrome and Bakelite necklace, 1972. *Barry Lategan*

Right page Long black and white opaque bead necklace, 1972. *David Bailey*

Far right A modern version of Art Deco – Ben Amun's jet and diamanté teardrop earrings, 1983. *Rico Puhlmann*

As raw materials for fine and costume jewelry became more and more expensive, many designers and consumers enthusiastically collected old and beautiful components from markets and junk shops. The decision by the United States government to deregulate the price of gold in August 1971 had an interesting effect on the costume jewelry market. Throughout the 1970s the price of gold had climbed, from $35 an ounce to an all-time peak of $850 an ounce in 1981. Designers turned to alternative materials because consumers could no longer afford fine metal jewelry. For a while there was an upsurge of interest in sterling silver jewelry, especially as greater sculptural artistry was invested in its design during this period. Tiffany's in New York was a pioneer in this work. However, by 1979, the price of sterling silver had also rocketed because the American speculator Nelson Bunker Hunt had attempted to corner the world silver market. Noble metals were now too expensive, and, inevitably, as cheaper forms of adornment were sought, many women turned to wearing costume jewelry.

Artists and artisans, working both in precious and non-precious materials, were patronized by new jewelry galleries which opened in many fashionable cities, such as London's Electrum and New York's Sculpture To Wear – the forerunner of Artwear. They promoted hand-crafted jewelry in limited editions as a collectable art form. Simplicity of form and the intrinsic characteristics of the materials were highlighted, at the expense of decorative detail. Following the bold and simple tradition of Georg Jensen's work, Elsa Peretti (who designed jewelry for the fashion minimalist Halston) and Paloma Picasso created a range of sterling silver jewelry.

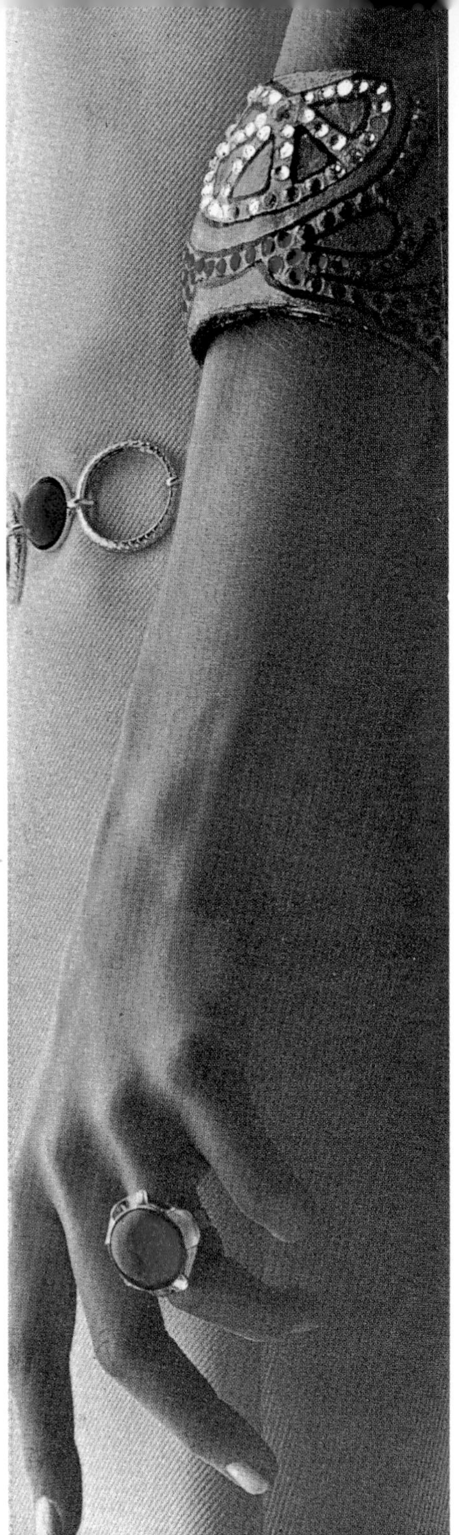

Far left Patricia von Muslin's tasselled cord and sculpted silver buckle on a cashmere dressing gown, 1982. *Barry Lategan*

Left Robert Lee Morris's 'corrugated' metal cuffs (for Artwear), 1986. *Albert Watson*

Opposite Chanel's 'gold finished' jewelry: bracelets, bangles, brooches and necklaces in faux-amber, -ruby, -emerald and -pearl piled on to a simple black pullover and on to a turban by Robertino for Severgnini, 1984. *Michel Comte*

PRECEDING PAGES

Left A splash of gold over a completely covered arm. Stephen Dweck's multi-chained, cluttered charm bracelet, with jade and tourmaline beads, and gold vermeil baskets, 1985. *Steven Meisel*

Centre left Siboa's gold-dipped *papier-mâché* armlet studded with faux-rubies and rhinestones; grand cardinal-red cabochon ring surrounded by curls of gold, worn with a finely wrought gilt belt interspersed with cabochon stones like dark sapphires, both by Adrian Mann, 1968. *Marc Leonard*

Centre right Elizabeth Gage's gilt finger rings and big, multicoloured stone rings wrapped round a belt at the wrist, 1986. *Steven Meisel*

Far right Wendy Gells's 'wristys' – extra-wide mock-gold filigree cuffs with square insets of green leather, 1985. *Steven Meisel*

Catherine Noll, Patricia von Muslin, Robert Lee Morris and Ted Muehling also concentrated on sculptural themes. Noll was the granddaughter of a sculptor, Alexandre Noll, who began to sculpt in wood in 1920. His signature was to carve from a single piece of wood rather than join together individual pieces, and he was renowned for his mastery of that material. Inspired by his work, Catherine Noll exhibited her first pieces of jewelry at her grandfather's retrospective in Paris in 1972. She concentrated on rounded, sculptural jewelry, using a variety of woods from the Southern hemisphere as well as ebony, ivory, plexiglass, stone, metal and granite.

Patricia von Muslin's sculptural jewelry, inspired by classical sculpture and architecture, was timeless. After designing the clay prototype, she made a mould to cast in metal, or carved the collection in wood or stone. One of her favourite materials was rock crystal, which attracted her because it was reputed to ward off evil.

Robert Lee Morris saw no distinction between his jewelry and his sculpture, just a difference of scale. Encouraged by the designs of Picasso, Calder, Man Ray and Louise Nevelson, which he saw exhibited at Sculpture To Wear, one of the first jewelry galleries in New York, he turned to jewelry making: 'I saw that the essence of the artist's work as I knew it had been successfully translated into wearable form. And the wearable form was so much more intimate than a painting. The fact that you could caress it, wear it, sleep with it... made it a more intimate and satisfying art to me.'

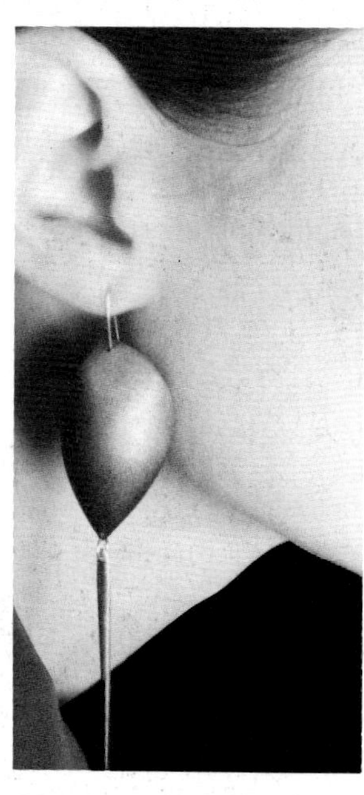

Top Cara Croniger's silver and multicoloured polyester resin earrings, 1980

Above Ted Muehling's pin-green niobium earring, electrically treated to achieve colouration, 1982. *Jim Varriale*

Opposite Black *objets trouvés* bowler hat hung with padlocks, safety pins and dog-lead clips, 1982. *Hans Feurer*

Mysticism and melancholy characterized Ted Muehling's jewelry. He based his designs on the unique shapes found in nature, creating abstract rather than literal interpretations of some of nature's elements: silver-, gold- or bronze-plated pod-shaped earrings, olive-pip bracelets, ginko-leaf hair ornaments and tiny, rice-grain earrings, 'like little punctuation marks'. Although he worked throughout the seventies with top fashion designers, including Calvin Klein and Issey Miyake, Muehling preferred to work on his own, and exhibited his work at Artwear.

The members of Artwear, set up in 1977, were constantly approached by major fashion designers to provide accessories for their collections. However, many members did not consider themselves costume jewelers, but rather artists working in the medium of jewelry, though some had worked with leading American and European fashion designers. The gallery's criterion for inclusion was that the artists pioneered the art of jewelry making, using materials in an unexpected and novel manner.

The work of the three founders, Robert Lee Morris, Ted Muehling and Cara Croniger, was on permanent exhibition: Croniger's resin and plastic jewelry in geometric, day-glo styles; Morris's voluptuous, glamorous metal jewelry in high gloss or mock-ancient patinas; and Muehling's naturalistic jewelry.

However extraordinary the designs were that were exhibited at Artwear, the pieces had to be wearable. Furthermore, the staff kept in close contact with magazines and clothes designers to guide their artists in a fashionable and thus commercial direction, if that was their wish.

Throughout the seventies less expensive materials were sought for decoration. The most extreme example of alternative adornment during this decade was provided by the Punks, who festooned themselves with creative salvage – safety pins, rubber tyre tubing and paper clips. They started a craze for jewelry that was, literally, 'junk': rubber, nuts and bolts, scraps of leather or cloth, bicycle chains, keys, buttons, bones and lavatory paper. The designers who marketed creative salvage jewelry were against craftsmanship, believing that too much emphasis on technique thwarted the spontaneity of a piece.

The wildest street culture fashion in London was on display at Cha Cha's, a one-night-a-week club run by Judy Blame and his friend Scarlett. Blame and Scarlett set the pace, appearing in Blame's oversized rubber fetishist jewelry. Blame was taken up by London fashion designers Anthony Price and John Galliano and by New York's Suzanne Bartsch, who imported the most avant-garde British fashion. They all liked and promoted his 'creative salvage'; buttons, Fimo plasticine figures, even rags and bones all found a place in his 'débris collages'.

Earring designers, in an attempt to solve the problem of weight in earrings, have frequently resorted to lightweight, hollowed-out metals, aluminium and man-made resins, on to which any patina can be applied.

Left Shooting-star gilt earrings by Mark Davis for Byzantium, 1985. *Andrea Blanch*

Below Hector Jorge's huge, gilt, gypsy-style triple earrings, 1971. *Irving Penn*

Opposite, far right Saint Laurent Couture's multitiered baroque gilt and stone drop earrings, 1980. *Peter Lindbergh*

Above Jean Shrimpton wears large, clip-on ball-and-chain earrings, 1967. *Peter Knapp*

Below Michael Hic's bold black and white crescent earrings of rhinestone-embedded wood, 1966. *Irving Penn*

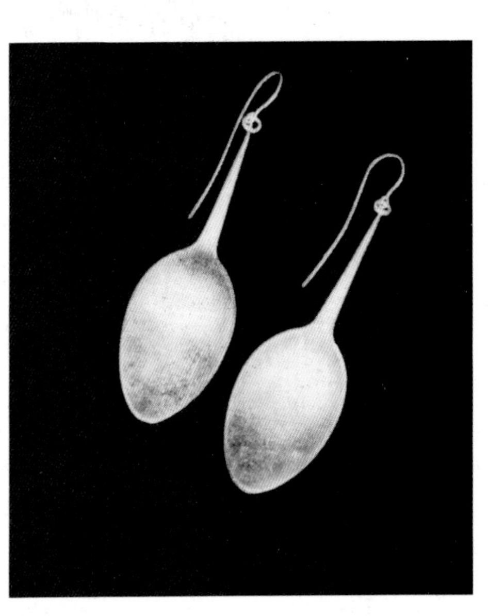

Similarly, the young Irish designer Tom Binns worked with *objets trouvés*, designing jewelry for numerous Vivienne Westwood collections: 'Clint Eastwood', 'Punkature', 'Witches' and fluorescent 'Savages'. His early work included fluorescent rubber jewelry and rubber buttons – looking like discarded chewing gum – and he later worked with Commes des Garçons and Rifat Ozbek. His figurative work, such as his bent brass wire ballerina figures, owed much to Calder, while Man Ray was probably an influence in the unexpected use of day-to-day articles like spoons or pen nibs soldered together to form a brooch.

Creative salvage jewelry was by its very nature one-off; no two pieces were identical. Gloria Lomas, who exhibited at Artwear, was often asked to make half a dozen copies of her lichen, tree bark, petrified wood or cactus root jewelry – the buyers being unable to grasp the fact that natural materials could not be mass produced. Lomas's work transcends fashion and achieves the rare distinction of becoming an art form. Her heavy, overpowering, hand-rolled leather cuffs studded with crystals were inspired by the bikers' culture; materials were often startlingly original: cactus roots and treebark collected in the country would be taken back to Harlem, backed with metal, protected with resin and turned into body sculpture; lichen fragments, fixed together to form a bracelet, were partly covered in gold-leaf, allowing the organic patina to show through. Much of her work was tinged with political and ecological messages; for instance, she designed an anti-human collection centred on the Chrysler Building in New York, which symbolized Manhattan's soulless sophistication.

The little black dress has maintained its position since the early 1920s as the indispensable wardrobe basic. Typically, it is a small, unadorned, well-cut dress in black cloth. Versatility is its strong point; it is always acceptable and fashionable, taking a woman through the day into the evening with a simple change of accessories. Consequently, it provides the perfect canvas on which a woman can paint her character; she can dress it up with dramatic costume jewelry or hide behind its understated anonymity. In the early 1980s the former style was ubiquitous – the little black dress highlighted with bold costume jewelry.

Opposite Inès de la Fressange wears classic Chanel: black bow and net, gilt earrings, with pearl and gilt chains around her waist and neck, 1984. *Daniel Jouanneau*

Opposite, above Tom Binns's 'spoon' earrings, and 'helping hand' clasping the waist, 1987. *Jeffrey Pendersen*

Right Saint Laurent's row upon row of hammered, gold-leafed metal, forming a collar and bracelet, 1972. *David Bailey*

Far right Pierre Taillées du Tyrol's coral, pearl and jet brooch provides the finishing touch to Givenchy's sheath dress, 1965. *William Klein*

Far left Valentino's astrakhan hat and matching red coat, worn with Billyboy's stone-encrusted resin 'heart-jewelry', 1985. *Steven Meisel*

Left Eric Beamon's jewelled mask, 1987

'Kitchen Sink', 'Gold Rush', 'Quick Silver', 'Go Ask Alice', 'The Eyes of Laura Mars' – these are some of the names given by the American designer Eric Beamon and his partners, Vicki Sarge and Robert Molnar, to their collage pieces in order to record their sources of inspiration. The team amassed old stocks of 1950s crystal or Venini glass beads, gewgaws, tin findings, ethnic trinkets, old or broken bits of jewelry picked up in New York and London markets – anything that glittered, or amused them. They strung these together with lavish exuberance. The effect was opulence without ostentation – one finds a simple sheath dress enhanced by a twinkling collar, or the hips of a pair of Levis heavy with thong-hung crystals.

The charm of Billyboy's jewelry, by contrast, was its naive crudity. Made of baked resin – originally cooked at home in the young American designer's oven – it was at once surreal, tribal and cartoon-like. 'I'm a product of the Flintstones,' he would say teasingly. He modelled the material, like a child moulding plasticine, into amorphous shapes which the most soigné women in the world, including Marie Hélène de Rothschild and Maxime de la Falaise, could flaunt. It had a sort of throw-away chic, the wit of Surrealism, of the misplaced, of the barbaric.

Billyboy's jewelry, lighthearted and yet deeply historical, was essentially modern. Painted in bright, crayon colours, studded with glass stones and randomly gold-leafed, it conjured up Stone-Age gingerbread men, ghouls, mock-candy in fancy wrappers and cartoon copies of Chanel's classic Maltese cross, coins and medallions.

In homage to his idol, Schiaparelli – 'My life is a dedication to her. I'm utterly, utterly in love with her' – Billyboy's work is full of allusions to Surrealism: painted resin eyes hung with teardrops recalling Dali's famous brooch (also reinterpreted by Stephen Dweck, a New York costume jewelry designer) or bright red lips hanging from snail shells. Refusing to regard costume jewelry as an art, he delighted in its ephemeral qualities. Leading fashion designers, such as Thierry Mugler, Hanae Mori and Diana von Fürstenberg, sought his collaboration.

Opposite left Saint Laurent's coloured resin rocks (developed by Goossens) in gilt settings for earrings, rings and bracelet, 1986. *Dominique Isserman*

Above right Jacques Gautier's long and light loop earrings in hand-painted resin resembling tortoise-shell, 1967. *Serge Lutens*

Below right Andrew Logan's 'Shwedagon' jewelry from his Burmese Collection, 1986: 22 carat gold-plated glass embedded in resin pagodas and bangles.

OVERLEAF

Left Butler and Wilson's period amber necklace and matching bracelets, 1972. *Barry Lategan*

Right Ernest Jackson's huge, tribal, painted wood cuff; Pellini's faux-amber stretch necklaces and bracelets for Callaghan; M. & J. Savitt's jasper and aragonite ball necklace; and Hidalgo's cornelian ball earrings, 1987. *Steven Meisel*

By the early eighties the costume jewelry market had expanded on both sides of the Atlantic. The prohibitive price of real, precious metals was not the only reason. Tom Binns stated categorically, 'Clothes are getting so boring that people have to accessorize themselves and the easiest way to do it is to buy costume jewelry.'

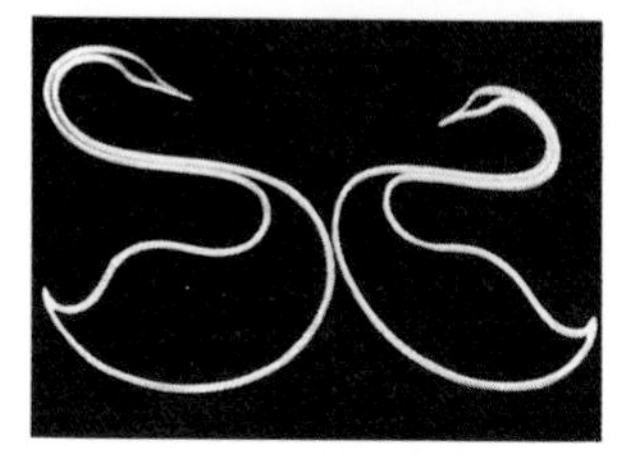

Top Tom Binns's 'prose pins', 1987. *Jeffrey Penderson*

Above Double swan brass brooch by Binns, 1986. *Neil Kirk*

Accessories, and specifically costume jewelry, gradually assumed greater importance in both women's and men's dress. While many jewelers were reluctant to be too closely associated with the clothing industry for fear of losing status and credibility, others were indignant that for so long fashion jewelry had been regarded only as a mere appendix by fashion designers, editors and customers alike. Apart from Chanel and Yves Saint Laurent, few had made jewels an intrinsic part of their 'look'.

With the revival of couture elegance, women wanted to savour the distinctive style of a favourite couturier; designer jewelry, scarves and bags were more sought after than ever. Women in the couture boutiques along the avenue George V or the via Condotti were seduced into browsing among the velvet upholstered tableaux displaying the 'little nothings' of the house.

During the last decade clothing prices have risen dramatically and women have spent more on their clothes – partly because they are particularly important to professional women. One solution has been to retain the classic lines for the actual clothing and to rely on seasonal accessories to provide the personal touch. Costume jewelry has assumed a much greater importance in the big couture collections, the details changing from season to season while the clothes themselves remained constant.

Above Chanel's intertwined double-C insignia earrings – a walking advertisement, 1986

The ubiquitous Chanel suit, a fashion classic, was recoloured by Karl Lagerfeld when he took over as designer-in-chief at Chanel Couture in 1982 and sanctioned the use of gilt, mock pearls and glass fakery. Haughty models came down Parisian catwalks wearing baroque pastiches of Chanel's original look on an essentially classic suit line. Chanel *bijoux* became the quintessential fashion theme of the early eighties, but Lagerfeld was actually parodying rather than recreating the gilt chain look of the fifties. He not only draped swags of chains, pearls and glass stones around his models' necks but also used the components of this jewelry as part of the clothing. Quilted leather mini-skirts were hung with chains in imitation of the classic Chanel bag, fabrics were printed with Chanel jewelry motifs and even the Chanel 'CC' insignia was made into enormous earrings and belts. These formed the ingredients of a huge promotion, which became further and further removed from Chanel's own notions of style.

Original Chanel jewelry became very collectable, partly because it was so beautifully made and had become a fashion classic, and partly because the

Opposite A fetishist's fantasy – tendrils of black rubber in a wig by Judy Blame, worn with Lesy's leather necklace, 1984. *Albert Watson*

Marshal Breslow's 'gold' flower-drop earrings for Calvin Klein, reminiscent of those worn by Monna Vanna, painted in 1866 by Dante Gabriel Rossetti, 1979. *Alex Chatelain*

prices paid at auctions were going steadily up. In 1982 Christie's in London held a sale of original Chanel jewelry which virtually fetched 'real' jewelry prices. One glass and gilt brooch, for example, was sold for £1,600. Costume jewelry was no longer what Chanel had intended it to be when she said: 'Women can wear fortunes that cost nothing.'

If contemporary costume jewelry was fashionably classic and well-made, then it became collectable. No more could it count as disposable ephemera. Pieces by Chanel, the Parisian Isabel Canovas, and the New Yorkers Robert Lee Morris, Stephen Dweck and Wendy Gells were the most sought after.

There was a distinct difference in attitude to costume jewelry between the designers in French houses and those in the United States. The French, and to a lesser extent the Italians, placed great importance on original accessories, investing time and money in evolving new ideas and materials. The Americans tended to rely on the collections presented by specialist shops such as Fragments, which showed the work of various jewelers, or to commission itinerant designers, merely demanding exclusives on certain pieces until after the show. In both cases, the designer was rarely credited and only a few houses considered jewelry to be integral to a season's look. British designers, too, apart from Vivienne Westwood and Jean Muir, treated costume jewelry as an afterthought.

Original costume jewelry was invariably prominent in Saint Laurent's collection. Working in collaboration with Louise de la Falaise, Goossens, Gripoix and the various craftsmen and artists who submitted both ideas and new materials, he crowned each collection with thematic costume jewelry. Louise de la Falaise observed that the more professional and experienced a designer or craftsman, the more avant-garde and daring he can afford to be. 'Bijoux Fantasie – it has to be crazy, fun, larger than life,' insisted de la Falaise. But, of course, the larger the piece, the heavier it was and a solution had to be found. In 1985 Saint Laurent went to China and brought back for de la Falaise some huge turquoises, which she decided to have copied by Goossens in a less weighty material. The latter developed a lightweight resin that could be moulded into any shape and size and assume various patinas.

Just as Louise de la Falaise worked side by side with Saint Laurent, so Arianne Brenner, as accessory designer at Ungaro, worked closely with this couturier from the very inception of a collection. Whereas at Chanel and Scherrer, jewelry was superimposed on to a look, at Ungaro pieces were designed from the beginning to reflect the theme of a collection; black resin hands might be pinned into the folds of the material or on to a waistband, or an asymmetrically slung necklace echo the diagonal cut of a bodice, their melancholy beauty reflecting the source of inspiration, in this case, the paintings of Gustav Moreau.

Opposite Isabelle Pascoe wears Saint Laurent's silver and diamanté hailstone earrings, 1985. *Snowdon*

Couture jewels are a product of the liaison between jewelry craftsmen and clothes designers. The aim is a unified look. In many cases the jewels become part of the actual gown.

Opposite, far left Issey Miyake's long, black wool jersey gown, with asymmetrical *décolleté*, trimmed with a coiled metal corselette, 1983. *George Hurrell*

Opposite, top Clerical Tessuto's elegant, low-backed black crêpe dress delineated by rows of gleaming rhinestone button-bows, 1986. *Javier Vallhonrat*

This page, above The stripes of Muir's cashmere kimono cardigan are echoed in Gary Wright and Sheila Teigue's yellow, blue and violet nylon bangle, 1985. *Eric Boman*

Above right Prince of Wales check ensemble, by Karl Lagerfeld, for Chloé, is enhanced by a spanner brooch with a pearl and diamanté bead at each end by Correani, 1983. *George Hurrell*

Right Jean Paul Gaultier's knitted cardigan and leggings worn with armloads of heavy bronze bracelets and a dramatic beret decoration – a collection of key chains hung with souvenirs, 1985. *Steven Meisel*

Left Stephen Dweck's clip-on earrings echo the dappled patina of Geoffrey Beene's flecked jacket worn also with Dweck's solid silver cuffs decorated with lizards in relief, 1986. *Irving Penn*

Above Oscar de la Renta's black velvet dress is decorated with a spray of sequinned and bejewelled medals, 1983. *Alex Chatelain*

Opposite Robert Lee Morris's big, bold, 'gold' accessories for Donna Karan – solid, 'curl' earrings, a collar of balls and chunky link and cuff bracelets, 1985. *Steven Meisel*

American designers favoured a simple, sports style that allowed for extravagant costume jewelry, and US women were bold enough to wear large, eye-catching pieces.

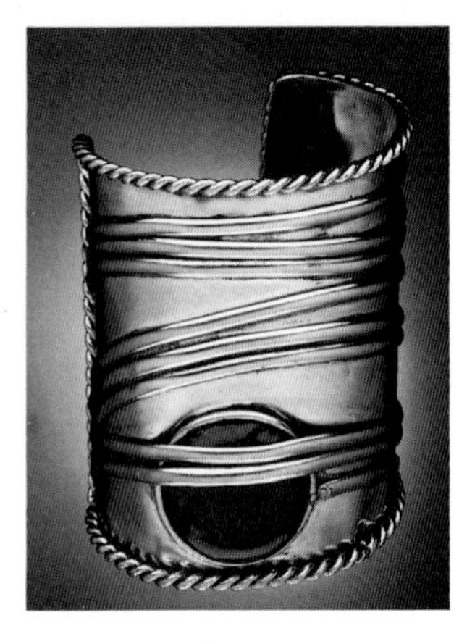

Far left Isabel Canovas's gilt chains hung with a turbaned head, 1986

Left Isabel Canovas's textured gilt cuff set with a semi-precious stone, 1986

Costume jewelry, as Dominique Sirop, Hubert de Givenchy's assistant, has pointed out, is a necessary loss leader in a couture collection since the cost of developing a prototype is so high in proportion to the number of pieces finally displayed. Sometimes up to fifty or sixty samples are made in one season and only a dozen or so subsequently used. Out of the experimentation and development undertaken for the couture, cheaper models in less expensive materials are mass produced each season for ready-to-wear collections.

Balenciaga's *directrice*, Madame Gilbert, considered that costume jewelry was in general a distraction; a perfect silhouette rendered it superfluous. The American fashion designer Geoffrey Beene, on the other hand, worked closely with many young designers, including Stephen Dweck, Arthur Colby and Cara Croniger, delighting in the way that worthless materials from down-and-out Canal Street, Manhattan, could be turned into accessories for thousand-dollar dresses. However, he refused to license his costume jewelry range because he believed that such pieces could not be mass produced without watering down their wit and provocative charm.

Donna Karan's simple, classic clothes came to life with the addition of Robert Lee Morris's costume jewelry. The two worked in close collaboration to present a range of accessories, transforming a daytime outfit to evening wear or updating a classic model.

Isabel Canovas commissioned, and in some cases revived, the work of artisans using leather, metal, semi-precious stones, *passementerie* and fur to create luxurious, high fashion accessories. After training in haute couture at the house of Dior, she left in 1982 to establish an haute couture accessory boutique – a new retailing notion. Each piece of jewelry was developed from original drawings and moulds (she rarely used findings) and could involve as many as eight different craftsmen for the different materials incorporated. The most noticeable characteristics of Canovas's jewelry were daring and bulk. She also enjoyed the noise it made when worn, the clank of gilt, the tinkle of beads or the crack of one galalith bangle against another.

Opposite Italian *Vogue's objets trouvés* of bogus jewels and everyday objects. Fake diamond and emerald drop earrings; Bianca e Blue's false diamond and sapphire brooch; Paolo Grioni's amber and silver oval brooch suspended from a safety pin – as are the keys – and green silk and plastic flowers pinned to the lapel, 1984. *Albert Watson*

OVERLEAF

Main picture The golden scrollwork of Patricia Lester's evening dress is echoed by Gloria Lomas's close-fitting honeycombed cuff made of gold-leafed tree bark and her matching lichen and tree bark earrings, 1986. *Sheila Metzner*

Below left Gold painted rocks on a knotted, frayed rope wound round a white evening glove, 1986. *Roxanne Lowit*

Below right Gloria Lomas's smoky driftwood, tangled wire and bauble earrings, 1985. *Arthur Elgort*

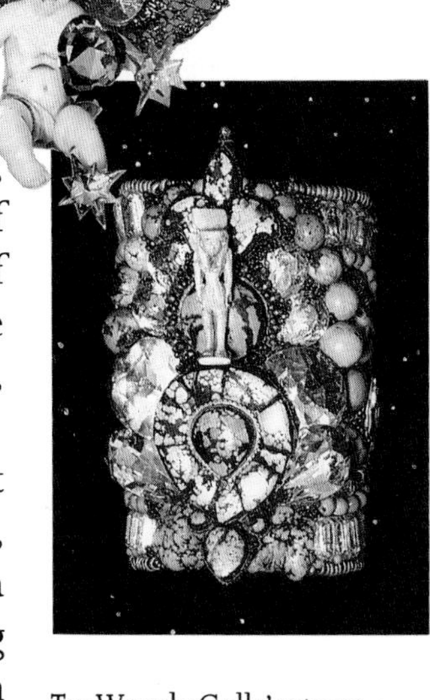

Wendy Gells's glue gun – an electric pressurized dispenser of fast-setting, strong adhesive – enabled her to create her collage jewelry. 'The principle of my designs' she stated, 'is to cover every available surface on a piece of jewelry' and she smothered cuffs, brooches, mirrors, drinking glasses, eye glasses and even Victorian dolls in a kaleidoscope of cut-glass stones, beads, plastic cherubs and leather.

'Gellmania' swept through the United States as people began to collect her one-off pieces at several thousand dollars each. Some of it was worn, some displayed as sculpture. One woman even used a Gells creation as a centrepiece for her dining table. A few pieces actually told a story: 'Landing Strip', a crystal and rhinestone necklace, depicted a runway with eleven planes overhead waiting to land. When Gells discovered that the bromeliad plant could be grafted onto tree bark and produce bright red flowers at Christmas time, she developed 'living' jewelry. 'Wristys' – her version of bracelets – necklaces and brooches were festooned with tendrils and blooms.

Top Wendy Gells's stone-studded and gilt-winged plastic cherub brooch, 1986

Above Wendy Gells's brass 'wristy', smothered in cut-glass stones, beads and *objets trouvés*, 1986

The jewelry of the Italian designer Donatella Pellini was as simple and refined as Gells's was cluttered. As a chemist and an artist, she mastered the manipulation and coloration of plexiglass, galalith and Rhodoid, creating a range of textures, such as speckled synthetic granite beads and geometric, boldly coloured mobiles. Her mock-amber, -cornelian, -coral and -ivory jewelry was famous for its convincing imitation, beauty, weightlessness and subtlety of colour.

Sandwiching layers of plexiglass between layers of glass, Pellini sliced through them to create a colour-graded cross section. She was inspired by her extensive collection of Bakelite jewelry, much of which had been designed by her grandmother, Emma Pellini. Donatella Pellini substituted Rhodoid and Perspex for Bakelite.

Donatella Pellini's accessories were given prominence by Versace, Gigli and Soprani. She appealed to the 'Renaissance' leanings of these leading Italian designers, but she was in fact a determined Modernist with a heightened sense of tradition. Gigli showed her ecological 'Green Line' of faux-amber, -tortoise-shell, -wood and -stone made of Rhodoid combined with Indian silver in 1986.

Above A selection of Donatella Pellini's 'Green Line' of faux-amber and -tortoiseshell, wood, metal and paste beads, 1987. *Steven Meisel*

Opposite Objets Trouvés – A pair of multicoloured glass bead belts slung round the waist of a mini-skirt, by Eric Beamon for Jasper Conran, 1986. *Patrick Demarchelier*

Dinny Hall, a pupil of Mick Milligan's at London's Central School of Art and Design, was inspired, like Pellini, by the simple clean lines prevalent in the 1920s. She bases other designs on architecture seen on her travels – such as the windows and tiles of the Alhambra in Southern Spain or Celtic stonework. Deriving her decorative themes from these, she simplifies the images, and working in wood and silver or anodized metal, produces endless permutations.

The stars of soap operas *Dynasty* and *Dallas* boosted the costume jewelry market – just as Hollywood had done in the thirties and forties. Some members of the British royal family, notably Princess Diana, adopted the 'soap opera look', combining fake and real jewelry, and contributed to a surge in the popularity of pearls.

The younger market followed the sartorial lead of their rock star heroes: Madonna, Cyndi Lauper, Michael Jackson and Boy George all popularized glittery paste. Holly Johnson of the pop group Frankie Goes To Hollywood told *Vogue* in 1984: 'People who don't wear costume jewelry have no future.' Certain pieces, worn by their idols, became classics for the youth market: Michael Jackson's crest pins, Richard Serbin's 'The King of Rock 'n' Roll' brooch worn by Madonna and Boy George, or Mera Poltan's cross and chain jewelry for Madonna. As leading male pop stars promoted 'gender-bending' clothes styles – wearing skirts, make-up and feminine accessories – their followers' meek imitation was to wear costume jewelry: a spangling brooch pinned proudly on a lapel.

By the early eighties every teeny bopper's denim jacket was pinned with a gaudy, diamanté pin or brooch; a Monty Don original or a copy. 'You can never be too obvious', said Monty Don, who with his partner Sarah Erskine encouraged men and women to wear obviously fake, paste jewelry: crystal drop earrings hanging from black satin bows, brash diamanté fish (a motif copied from Sarah's cookbook) and lizards; heavy, black lacquered punk chains; and the rosewood and bone jewelry based on Barbara Hepworth sculptures. The latter appeared as accessories in a Betty Jackson collection.

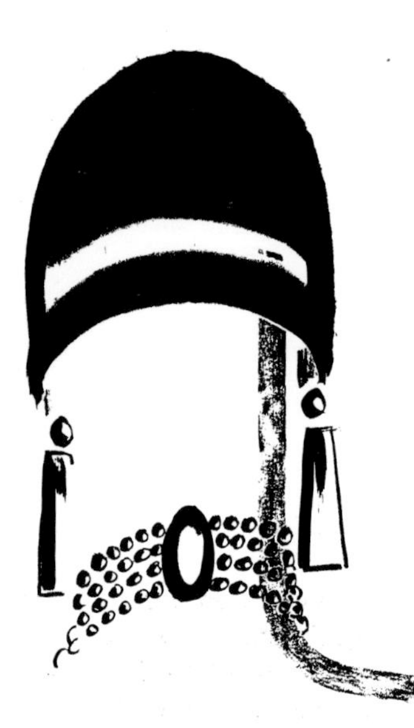

Monty Don's smoked glass earrings and black glass choker for Bruce Oldfield, 1983. *Tony Viramontes*

Costume jewelry is a lucrative commodity, with a large profit margin. Since the 1960s, manufacturers have become more and more aware of the changing nuances of fashion, gearing their production and distribution to keep pace with the various season's clothing, some offering five or six ranges a year. Several old factories and ateliers specializing in virtually extinct crafts have been reopened.

Gradually the public gained a greater appreciation of the technicalities of jewelry making and demanded better quality, for which it was prepared to pay. Realizing that styles repeated themselves, people now tended to keep, rather than throw out, their old pieces.

By the late eighties the fashion world had reacted against flashy, glitzy jewelry. Stronger, simpler, more sculptural pieces were promoted, exemplified by the work of Robert Lee Morris, Barry Kieselstein-Cord, Isabel Canovas and M. & J. Savitt. The grey tones of metals – silver, pewter, steel and alloys – treated to create unusual textures and patinas outmoded the garish attractions of coloured paste jewelry. In London, a number of young designers experimented with patina and finish, creating a variety within this

Gary Wright and Sheila Teigue's four-hoop silver earrings worn with 22 matching bangles, 1985. *Patrick Demarchelier*

narrow colour range. Julian Brogden of Atelier favoured unplated matt metals inspired by the sculpture of Brancusi and the shapes of broadcasting equipment of the 1940s. James Cox perfected an electro-technique which coated plastic objects in metal. He played with verdigris finishes. David and Kulip Millman's bold geometric shapes were worked in matt and gloss aluminium, alloys, chrome and pewter.

'Real-looking' as well as real jewelry came back into fashion, such as green-patina, mock-gold effects; intaglios and seals; vermeil (silver plated with gold); and opulent, Bulgari-style pieces that could be worn by day and night as a sort of identity mark. Quality was consequently as important as appearance; the back of a piece had to be finished as carefully as the front, the stones set – rather than glued – into the claws, the clasps finely polished and the gilt carefully finished.

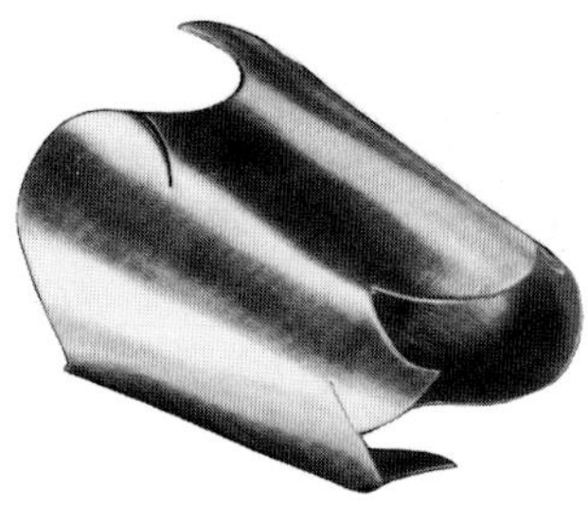

Above Stephen Dweck's curvy, matte finished sterling silver cuff, 1986. *Irving Penn*

Below Barry Kieselstein-Cord's 18-carat-gold estate jewelry rings and Rosecraft's 'gold' hoop earrings, 1986. *Wayne Maser*

Even today the techniques for making costume jewelry remain very old fashioned. The production of original, top quality pieces is still time-consuming – casting, moulding, gilding and stone-setting are done by hand – and has changed very little since the beginning of the century. In the troisième arrondissement of Paris, for example, sweatshops still produce findings in a manner virtually unchanged since the nineteenth century. Entering one of the grey stone buildings which house the findings companies, one is met by the sound of thunderous pounding. The showroom is lined from floor to ceiling with magnificent Victorian mahogany drawers, like stacks of wooden treasure chests, each embossed with a tarnished tin finding, indicating its contents.

In the workshops behind, a cloud of powder and metal filings hangs in the air. Amid the dry dust and relentless crashing stand a row of half-naked men, poised in front of stamping machines. These are the source of the noise. With the left hand a thin plate of tin or metal alloy, two by three inches, is placed down on a flat grinding stone; with the right hand a leather strap suspended from the ceiling, a 'cow's tongue', is grasped, heaved down, thereby lifting an enormous stone weight, and released to slice the imprint into the tin plate beneath. This motion is repeated again and again, perhaps thirty times a minute, and the finding thrown into a waiting basket. From there it is taken across the room to a row of pinafored women hunched over polishing wheels, each personalized with a prayer card of the Virgin Mary or a family photograph. Unprotected by a mask or simple handkerchief from the flying debris, they clean the rough edges of the findings against rotating lathes. These tin components are then stored in the drawers in the showroom and sold by the kilo to be gilded, painted or inlaid with stones by costume jewelers.

With the renaissance of the couture, traditional craftsmen have found their skills in greater demand and the relative affluence and increased demand have made their precision craft affordable once again.

Costume jewelry is inevitably dependent upon fashion; jewelry conceived without regard for fashion is sterile. Costume jewelry can play various roles. It can be a joke, a talking point, a note of identity, a classic touch or an exercise in sheer drama. But while no one worries any longer about wearing 'imitation', some women have now become so preoccupied with the value of 'antique' costume jewelry that they do not wear it with the necessary light touch. They miss the point, that it is, by its very nature, ephemeral. They would do better to take Simon Wilson's sound advice:

'Stuff signatures, just enjoy wearing it.'

Opposite James Cox's chemically patinaed copper-mesh hat, fixed with gold-plated steel and nickel pins, and his electro-formed copper bangles, 1987. *Bill Batten*

Glossary

Acrylic Plastic material used since the early 1970s, in rod, sheet or liquid form, which is cut or melted into shape

Aigrette Hair or hat ornament which is either shaped like a feather or holds the stem of a feather. Popular before the First World War

Amber Fossilized natural resin from pine trees

Anodizing Process by which the outer, oxidized layer of metal is dyed

Baguette Gemstone cut in a semi-circular section

Bakelite First truly synthetic plastic, made from formaldehyde and phenol, invented in 1907/9 by Leo Hendrick Baekeland, a Belgian chemist living in the United States. Produced in England from 1919. International heyday in the 1920s and 1930s

Berlin Iron Jewelry Patriotic jewelry made of highly intricate, blackened, high carbon cast iron, produced in Germany during the 19th century and again during the Great War. Introduced during the 1813-15 War of Liberation, it was given in exchange for fine jewelry, which was used to subsidize the war effort

Blanketing The catching of ore in suspension by a blanket sluice

Bohemian Glass Hand-made glass, often coloured, made in Northern Czechoslovakia

Bois Dulci *See* **Jet**

Brilliant Stone cut with 58 facets

Bugle Beads Tube-shaped glass beads used for decoration on dresses

Cabochon Stone cut with smooth surface, without facets

Calibré Cut Oblong or ellipitical cut to stone

Cameo Stone with two different coloured layers, usually onyx, agate or sardonyx, in the upper of which a figure is carved in relief

Casting Process of pouring molten metal into a mould to assume a shape when cool

Centrifugal/Investment/Lost Wax Casting Process of mass-production casting whereby a hand-made metal model is enclosed in a vulcanized rubber casing which is then split in two. The metal is removed and the space filled with molten wax to make a wax model. The wax model is then placed in a metal container and covered with plaster of Paris, the 'investment'. When the wax is heated and runs away a hollow mould is left. This mould is placed in a centrifuge and molten metal is poured in to form metal replicas of the original metal model

Chasing Embossing or engraving the surface of metalwork in relief

Chip Stone Small piece chipped or cut from a gemstone

Claw Setting Style of setting in which the gem is held in place by a series of vertically projecting claws folded down over the stone's edges to grip it to its setting

Cloisonné Form of enamelling whereby compartments are made with thin plates set on edge upon a foundation plaque and into these variously coloured, powdered enamels are poured, which are then fused

Crystal Rock crystal (durable quartz). Clear, transparent mineral, reputed to ward off evil. Crystal can be deeply etched using a simple drill, a slurry of diamond dust and olive oil

Cultured Pearls *See* **Pearls**

Cut Steel Jewelry Stud or head-shaped cut steel, faceted and density-set for brilliance

Diamanté Material set with rhinestones or other non-precious stones that sparkle like diamonds

Enamel Semi-opaque, coloured glass covering made from powdered and fused glass

Essence d'Orient Composition of fish scales and parchment size used to coat the surface of synthetic pearls

Filigree Type of metalwork made of plain, twisted or plaited fine metal wire

Fish Pearls *See* **Pearls, Imitation**

Foil Thin sheet of coloured metal alloy mounted behind a gem to enhance its colour

Fool's Gold *See* **Marcasite**

French Jet *See* **Jet**

Galalith An ammonia, hydrogen and carbon dioxide based plastic developed by Adolf Spittler and W. Krische in Germany in 1897. Galalith was commercially available in Britain by 1919 under various names, e.g.: Lactoid, Dorcasine and Keronyx

Gilding Process of covering any material with a thin layer of gold or gold alloy. Traditionally, gold dust was mixed with mercury and painted on. The mercury evaporates and a layer of gold is left

Electro-gilding Early-19th-century innovation which came into practice only in the late 19th century to replace mercurial-gilding which was considered dangerous. Produces a microscopically thin layer of gold, usually 24 carat, which tends to wear off quickly

Electro-plating The electrical process, using an anode and a cathode, by which gold is transferred through an acid cyanide base

Rolled Gold Gold which is laminated onto a surface. Introduced in 1817 and succeeded in the late 1950s by hard gold plating – a more controlled process which produced plating of a high standard

Gilding Metal *See* **Pinchbeck**

Imitation Gems *See* **Crystal, Diamanté, Glass, Marcasite, Paste, Strass**

Imitation Jet *See* **Vulcanized Rubber; Jet, French**

Imitation Pearls *See* **Pearls, Imitation**

Intaglio Engraving or carving below the surface of an object to give the impression of a design in relief

Iron Pyrites *See* **Marcasite**

Jet Very light, fossilized driftwood, found in seams 1-6 inches thick, parallel to shale deposits, which polishes to a high black lustre

French Jet Imitation of the above, which is heavier and cold to touch. Made from glass-covered wax

Vulcanized Rubber Imitation jet, made from sulphur and heat-treated

India rubber, invented by the American Charles Goodyear in 1838. It was patented in England in 1856 by Thomas Hancock

Marcasite Fool's gold or iron pyrites. Oxidized iron highly polished to imitate diamonds, and mounted in a pavé setting in silver or other metals. Revived for Edwardian shoe buckles, replacing the earlier technique of cut steel. Unlike paste, marcasite is cut like a gem and set into claws

Niello Silver decorated with a dark grey metallic inlay

Paillette Decorative spangle on dress

Parure Matching set of necklace, brooch, bracelet and earrings. A demi-parure is a pair of matching pieces. A parure can also refer to a jewelled collar and cuff set attached to a dress

Paste Glass used to imitate gems. Cheaper than marcasite and set into stampings rather than individual claws. *See also* **Strass** *and* **Rhinestone**

Pâte de Verre Glass paste. Ground glass mixed with a fluxing medium, and then melted and coloured. The technique was invented by the ancient Greeks and revived in 19th-century France

Patina The discolouration which occurs in certain metals when they are exposed at length to the atmosphere and which produces a thin, greenish layer on the surface of copper and bronze, or a reddish effect on gold. Acids can create this effect artificially

Pavé Setting Style of setting in which the surface of the jewelry is closely paved with stones, usually in clusters of seven, each touching the others

Pearls

Cultured Pearl Pearl produced artificially by implanting an irritant into an oyster shell. Perfected in 1914 by Mikimoto in Japan

Imitation Pearl Fish, Roman or fake pearl, made from a wax-filled glass ball coated with a pearly skin

Seed Pearl Tiny pearl, real or fake, used in jewelry and embroidery

Perspex I.C.I. proprietary name for Plexiglass, or Lucite, a petroleum-based, synthetic material

Pinchbeck Gilding metal. Copper zinc alloy (80-90 percent copper) similar to gold. Although it is golden in colour, pinchback is not a perfect match to gold, so is usually given a gold veneer

Plexiglass Polymercerized methyl methacrylate, a tough, transparent thermoplastic that is much lighter than glass and does not splinter

Plique à Jour Enamelling effect similar to that of a stained-glass window, whereby a metal frame design is filled in with variously coloured, translucent enamels

Prose Jewelry Jewelry decorated with a word or sentence

Resin Solid organic substance extracted from pine or fir trees, often used for beads

Rhinestone Imitation diamond made from glass (paste)

Rhodoid Proprietary name for the incombustible thermoplastic derived from cellulose acetate

Rolled Gold *See* **Gilding**

Roman Pearl *See* **Pearl, Imitation**

Sautoir Long necklace, usually extending to below the waist, often with a tassel or pendant suspended from the bottom

Seed Pearls *See* **Pearls, Seed**

Sequin Tiny, shiny metal or plastic disc which can be dyed and sewn onto a garment or accessory for decorative effect

Simulated Pearls *See* **Pearl, Imitation**

Strass Brilliant type of paste, used for imitation stones, developed by the Parisian royal jeweler Georges-Frédéric Strass in 1780

Vermeil Sterling silver plated with a fine layer of gold

Vrais Bijoux en Toc Name given to Chanel's collection of costume jewelry

Index

Page references in *italics* refer to illustrations and captions